A ROMAN CATHOLIC IN THE WHITE HOUSE

A Roman Catholic In The White House

BY JAMES A. PIKE

IN COLLABORATION WITH RICHARD BYFIELD

GREENWOOD PRESS, PUBLISHERS
WESTPORT, CONNECTICUT

The Library of Congress has catalogued this publication as follows:

Library of Congress Cataloging in Publication Data

Pike, James Albert, Bp., 1913-1969.
    A Roman Catholic in the White House.

    Bibliography: p.
    1.   Church and state in the United States.
2. Catholic Church in the United States. 3. Presidents
--United States--Election--1960. I. Title.
[BR516.P5 1972]   261.7   72-7508
ISBN 0-8371-6514-8

Originally published in 1960
by Doubleday & Company, Inc., Garden City, New York

Reprinted with the permission of
Doubleday & Company, Inc.

First Greenwood Reprinting 1972

Library of Congress Catalogue Card Number 72-7508

ISBN 0-8371-6514-8

Printed in the United States of America

Foreword

THE LAST TIME this question came up, I was clear in my convictions. I was for Al Smith. It was not because he was a "wet," as they called it then: I wasn't much interested in drinking. I was only seventeen. It was because he was a Roman Catholic. The diocesan paper I read—and swore by—was all for him, and I felt that the election of a Roman Catholic as President would do much to advance the cause of the Church to which I was devoted. More than that, I was disgusted—and personally hurt—by the heavy barrage of prejudiced and bigoted propaganda against my Church, which, while not issued officially by the Republican Party, was widely tolerated by it, and which at the time I suspected was encouraged by it.

As you have already gathered, I could not vote (not that my one vote would have mattered in staying the heavy defeat Mr. Smith endured). Nevertheless, I was not inactive. I talked up the Smith cause to adults inside my Church and out. I found particularly intransigent a Roman Catholic aunt. She, along with her non-Catholic husband, was for Mr. Hoover. I sought for some weeks to persuade her that, out of loyalty to her Church, she should switch her allegiance. In fact, the night before the election I drove up to her house in my Model T Ford to seek another opportunity of persuasion. They were out, and the best I could do was to leave a note with a simple inscription: "Remember to vote for Al Smith." She didn't.

Thirty-two years have passed. Though, in the meanwhile, I majored in political science in college, became a lawyer, served the government, studied theology, was ordained a Catholic priest (but in a different Communion from that in which I started) and on the side taught Church-State relations for six years at Columbia Law School—after all this, I still do not know whether Mr. Smith would have made a better President than Mr. Hoover. The Depression came near the end of the Presidential regime in question and it is a matter of speculation as to whether Mr. Smith's policies could have averted it; in any case one thing is clear, had they not, it all would have been blamed on the Roman Catholic Church!

But two things I do know from my study and thought in the intervening years: (1) I was quite wrong in simply wanting a Roman Catholic as such (in this my equally loyal Roman Catholic aunt was right); and (2) wrong also were those who wanted to bar Al Smith from office simply because he was a Roman Catholic. Therefore, now that the issue has been raised again, I feel called to say something on the matter, not only because of my past experience with this issue but because of the blessing of preparation in both law and theology and the experience of devotional nurture in two religious communions (both of which I have been enthusiastic about and critical of at various times up to the present) and my sympathy with the secular mind—due to my experience of being, between the two religious allegiances, an "agnostic."

None of this goes to prove that what is said in the pages which follow is altogether right; it is simply support for the fact that we do not mean it to be prejudiced or biased. As for Roman Catholics, those in this state, at least, will remember that publicly I fought rather hard alongside them, and in all mass media, to defeat the proposition supported by many Protestants and secularists to provide a discriminatory tax against parochial schools (and this at a time when the schools of our own Diocese were, unfortunately, scant); and as for Protestants and secularists, they will recall from the press and newsmagazines that I have just emerged from the struggle of the foreign aid-birth control issue, which was brought to the level of national politics and foreign policy by the Thanksgiving Day statement of the Roman Catholic Bishops. My stand on these two issues (it has been my lot in recent years on issues to have different bedfellows each time) should be at least a reassurance as to our intention of objectivity in the present analysis.

This endeavor had its inception in the request to me from the editors of *Life* which resulted in the article in the issue of December 21, 1959, entitled "A Catholic for President?" Of course, because of the necessary limitations of space, it was not possible there to spell out completely the background and implications of this issue; but, since all of the material in the article finds its place here, I am grateful to the editors and research assistants of *Life* who made a contribution to the clarity of expression and the verification of data.

In this larger work, the Rev. Canon Richard Byfield, who, for the article, had been kind enough to assist in some of the research, has become a collaborator, sharing in the writing. Because of his theological acumen and historical sense, no less than his journalistic background, he has contributed much to our joint endeavor: hence, the "we" used in the succeeding chapters is not simply the traditional episcopal "we"; it is meant to express joint thinking and writing.

I am happy to have this opportunity, in connection with the publication of a book in this field, to say how rewarding was my collaboration in the seminar in Church-State relations at Columbia Law School, first with Professor Noel T. Dowling, and for the last four years before coming to California, with Professor Harry W. Jones. Helpful, too, in connection with statements by Cardinal Ottaviani and Fr. Murray (Chapters Three and Four), was a paper written by one of the students in the seminar, Don Antonio Márquez.

Canon Byfield and I are most appreciative of the careful assistance in research, and the suggestions, of one of my priests, the Rev. Gerard P. Mundy, M.A., S.T.L. (Catholic University of America), formerly chaplain to American Roman Catholic students at the Sorbonne and presently Vicar of St. Aidan's Church, San Francisco. I am especially grateful to my wife for her patience, as, in the midst of many other ecclesiastical duties, I undertook another book, and for her advice on the subject matter itself and her care in checking the manuscript. We also wish to thank the members of our staff who put in much extra effort in recent months in this and cognate matters—the *Life* article, many letters on it and on the foreign aid-birth control issue, and the typing of these pages: Miss Margaret Cowans, Miss Marion Holtom, Mrs. David Graham, and Mrs. Ruth Dunavon. I am also grateful to hundreds of citizens of every faith who, during the foreign aid-birth control discussion and after the publication of my article in *Life*, through their letters (including the usual "negative fan mail") provided an amazing cross section of American opinion on these vital issues. Canon Byfield and I answered all the letters, though many of them, of necessity, briefly; our correspondents will find a fuller answer in this volume but also find that they have helped inform these pages.

JAMES A. PIKE

The Cathedral Close, San Francisco
Feast of St. John the Evangelist, 1959

Contents

A ROMAN CATHOLIC IN THE WHITE HOUSE

CHAPTER ONE

Bigotry? A Religious Test?

IT HAS BEEN more than thirty years since the country was divided over a religious issue in a Presidential campaign. A new generation of voters has arisen, most of whom would deprecate the excesses which surrounded the Presidential campaign of Alfred E. Smith in 1928. Many articles published in recent months have suggested that the era of religious bigotry is dead and that nothing like this could ever happen again. The temper of the electorate would, by and large, seem to indicate that this is so. Even the political parties, notoriously cautious on the question of a Roman Catholic candidate for President, have apparently lost much of the fear which was instilled into them by the Smith campaign. In the Democratic party a Roman Catholic Senator has come to the fore as a leading Presidential possibility; the Republican party, which seems to have no Roman Catholics in sight as Presidential timber, has at least one in the wings as a possible Vice-Presidential candidate. Both parties have expressed the hope that if their nominees are Roman Catholics this fact will not become an issue in the election. As a matter of fact, the Senator referred to above recently managed to put "reverse English" on the question. Some have asked whether nomination of a Roman Catholic would hurt the party; the Senator has publicly stated that a failure to nominate him because of his religion will damage the party.

Actually, it is hard to assess the actual effect of Al Smith's Roman Catholicism on the election in 1928. It is perfectly obvious that he lost the election; and, indeed, lost it by a far greater margin than might normally have been expected. Of course, other factors had their part to play. Chief among these was the "wet/dry" issue. Smith was an

avowed wet, and while Prohibition was far more widely honored in
the breach than in the observance, especially in the large Eastern
cities, apparently the country was not yet ready to vote "wet." The
fact that just five years later Prohibition was repealed does suggest,
however, that probably by 1928 the prohibitionist power was waning.
It is almost certain that the prohibitionists could not have defeated
Al Smith—without the religious issue to assist them.

As a result of the Al Smith contest, the until then Solid South was
broken wide open. States which had not chosen Republican electors
since the Reconstruction period were suddenly found in the Republican column. Party lines were crossed as men who had been voting
Democratic since the first Bryan campaign cast their first Republican
vote. The so-called "Catholic vote," which some had predicted would
put Al Smith in the White House, proved to be not effective—if,
indeed, it existed at all.

How Large Was the Issue?

Some writers have pointed out that it is very unlikely that any
Democrat could have won in 1928, regardless of his religion or his
views on Prohibition. The scandal-ridden Harding administration had
been succeeded by the do-nothing administration of Calvin Coolidge.
But this sort of "do-nothingism" represented for many the "normalcy"
for which they had been looking under Harding. Some observers were
predicting that catastrophe was imminent, but the upward-spiraling
business cycle of the Coolidge administration seemed to give them
the lie. Things were going well, and there did not seem to many any
reason for making a change.

On the other hand, impartial observers have pointed out that as
between Smith and Hoover the choice was rather plain. Smith was
believed by many of his contemporaries to be one of the outstanding
statesmen on the American scene. From his humble beginnings on
New York's lower East Side, he had risen to become a most effective
Governor of New York State. Even those who doubted his background
experience could not but admit that his political growth in the various
positions he had held had been phenomenal. He had outgrown not
only his poverty-ridden beginning but also his early involvement with
Tammany Hall. Although this latter connection was used strongly
against him in the campaign, the fact was that everyone who knew
him realized that he was not beholden to that organization.

While it is impossible, therefore, to assess the real reasons for Al Smith's defeat, all agree that one of the major factors in the campaign was the question of his religion. There were several periods during the campaign when this seemed like *the* issue. One remembers the circular letter written by Mrs. Willie W. Caldwell, Virginia National Committeewoman, in which she called upon her fellow Republican women to "save the United States from being Romanized."[1] The colorful Mrs. Mabel Walker Willebrandt, who was actually an Assistant Attorney General of the United States at the time she called upon Methodists throughout the land to unite to keep Governor Smith from the White House, was herself responsible for a great deal of the attention which the press gave to the religious issue. America in 1928 was asked a number of questions, but high among them was the question, "Do you want a Roman Catholic President?" In 1928, at least, she was prepared to answer this question with a resounding "No."

However, neither party came out of the election with clean hands. The Democratic party, still making capital with the epithet "Rum, Romanism and Rebellion," had attempted to see what it could do through using the first two words in the epithet as assets, as it had done in the Cleveland-Blaine campaign. The party had made a real effort to attract the "Catholic vote" and to attract enough more support from non-Catholic "wets" to put their man in office. The Roman Catholic Church in 1928 was still very much the Church of the immigrant. The Democratic party made a shameless pitch for the support of these immigrants, and it must be said that it was supported in this approach by many immigrant priests. It was reported at the time that from the pulpit of many Roman Catholic parishes as well as in the Church press Al Smith was frankly supported; the people were urged to vote for him simply because he was a Roman Catholic. By the same token, in many Protestant pulpits and publications the reverse position was taken and Protestants were urged to vote against Smith on the dual grounds of his Roman Catholicism and his espousal of the "wet" cause.

The Republicans, meanwhile, disclaiming any appeal to religious prejudice at the official level, did not take any steps to alienate the support they were receiving from those who were motivated by religious bigotry. Many "unofficial" publications, which made a straightforward appeal to anti-Roman Catholic prejudice, were, at least by default, supported by the Republican party and allowed to be circulated by party workers. Mrs. Willebrandt's activities, already referred to, are significant here. It is safe to say that few voters in 1928 were unmoved—in one direction or the other—by the religious affiliation of Mr. Smith.

How Important Is the Question Now?

The question has more or less lain dormant through the intervening years. No Roman Catholic has appeared as a serious Presidential contender, although Senator Kennedy of Massachusetts made a most dramatic bid for the Vice-Presidential spot on the Democratic ticket in 1956. The old wounds have been forgotten, the enmities which flared up during the Smith campaign have been allowed to die. But increasingly, in view of the present political situation and its possibilities, the questions are beginning to come up again.

Fortunately, it is unlikely that the questions will ever be raised in the same way. One of the prime factors in the 1928 campaign was the Ku-Klux Klan, which wielded great power in both parties—so great that most politicians of the day were unwilling to disclaim or condemn it. Also, the issue of "Americanism" was still strong, and Governor Smith was seen as a representative of the "upstart" immigrant people who were trying to rise above their "proper station in life." This question surely cannot arise in 1960. Finally, Prohibition, his public opposition to which was so damaging to Governor Smith, is, of course, no longer an issue. The picture is quite different. And yet the question is still before us, "Should a Roman Catholic become President of the United States?"

As of the time of writing, Senator Kennedy was one of the front runners for the Democratic nomination, and another Roman Catholic, Governor Edmund G. Brown of California, was also a possibility. With two men of such stature in the picture it seems very likely that one or the other of them will be a candidate at least on the Vice-Presidential level. It seems safe to say that no party will attempt to produce a ticket with two Roman Catholics on it. If Senator Kennedy is nominated for the Presidency, Governor Brown will certainly not be a Vice-Presidential candidate. However, should one of the other Presidential possibilities be chosen to lead the ticket, the likelihood of a Roman Catholic Vice-Presidential nominee, namely, either

Senator Kennedy or Governor Brown (or perhaps Governor Mike DiSalle of Ohio) will become very strong indeed.

There is also the possibility that both parties would include a Roman Catholic on the ticket. Prominent among Republicans is James Mitchell, Secretary of Labor, and others have been mentioned. Many observers have felt that if one party nominated a Roman Catholic for either office, the other party may feel obliged to do the same. This would be by way of an appeal to the so-called "Catholic vote" which, whether real or not, is still considered to be important by those who direct the practical party politics of our nation.

Of course, the question is the same, no matter how the ticket lines up. If a man is elected Vice-President he is, ex officio, the President of the Senate; and equally importantly, he is the potential President of his country. While we shall not take up space as we proceed to mention "Presidents and Vice-Presidents," we say now for the record that anything here said about the President can be said with equal truth about the Vice-President. If there are any dangers in the election of a Roman Catholic President, they are equally (although, perhaps, not so immediately) inherent in the election of a Roman Catholic Vice-President.

Is the Question Bigotry?

The first question that the very publication of such a book as this will raise in the minds of many is, "Does not your talking about such a question put you in the camp of the bigots?" The religious temper of mid-twentieth-century America is such that anyone even so much as breathing such a concern is liable to classification as a bigot. The man in the street, it appears, firmly believes that "What your religious faith is doesn't matter so long as you are sincere." In the minds of some people the raising of any religious question, in any context, smacks of bigotry—and "to inject the question of religion into politics" is bigotry, per se. This book is being written not to further the cause of bigotry but in an effort to help avert it. There is real danger that the Al Smith drama may be re-enacted with a different *dramatis personae*. It is our feeling that the most effective way to overcome unreasoning prejudice is to debunk the false questions, to ask the real questions, and to bring the real issues out into the open where they may be discussed. If to raise religious questions at all is bigotry, then, of course, this is a bigoted book; but if, as we believe, religious questions have a definite place in the political life of our country, and if this place can be defined and the questions themselves examined, then we feel bigotry can be avoided and sensible discussion can take its place. If a Roman Catholic is nominated for the Presidency feelings will run high. Our sincere purpose is to channel these feelings into their proper and logical paths and to help our citizens to understand what the questions implied by a candidate's religious beliefs really are.

Many people are aware of the existence of religious and racial bigotry without ever having understood the dynamic which lies behind it. There is a real sense in which prejudice of this type is a "semantic" problem. That is to say, the bigot is a person who believes in the existence of categories of people and believes that these categories are determinative in understanding the people or events categorized. An essential element of religious bigotry is that the bigot believe that a statement beginning "All Roman Catholics are . . ." is a possible and logical statement. When a person begins to realize that such statements are nearly always useless and generally dangerous, he is well on the road to overcoming his temptation to prejudice. It is an interesting exercise to try to think of a statement beginning with the word "all" which is literally true. In the racial field, for instance, many people have come to understand their antipathy toward Negroes better by trying to find an adjective which applies to all Negroes. Obviously, not even the word "black" will suffice—at least not in a Southern society in which a person with even a small proportion of Negro blood is considered to be a "Negro." All Negroes are not black, all Orientals are not inscrutable, all Jews are not sharp businessmen, all Scotsmen are not parsimonious—and so on, *ad infinitum*. By the same token, there is no adjective which applies to *all* Roman Catholics.

The Roman Catholic Bishops, in their Thanksgiving Day proclamation on the subject of the use of foreign-aid funds to help nations with population-control problems would have done well to remember this. Much heat would have been dissipated had their statement not implied that they were declaring what all Roman Catholics would oppose.

To the best of our knowledge, there is no one statement which can be made about Roman Catholics in general which would apply to every Roman Catholic in particular. But the bigot and the prejudiced person overlook this fact. "All Catholics are more loyal to the Pope than to their own country" is a statement designed to incite immediate agreement from altogether too large a segment of our population. "All Catholics would vote for a Roman Catholic for President" is a statement which is demonstrably false. It may be that enough Roman Catholics would vote for a Roman Catholic candidate to make the "Catholic vote" a reality. Even this, however, is by no means certain.

A "Catholic Vote?"

James M. O'Neill, in *Catholicism and American Freedom* (an answer to Paul Blanshard's book, *American Freedom and Catholic Power*), throws some light on the question of a Roman Catholic vote.[2] He summarizes the voting record of the Eightieth Congress on fifteen separate bills. The records in the Senate range all the way from that of Senator McGrath, Democrat of Rhode Island, who voted favorably on all the bills save one, to that of the late Senator Joseph McCarthy, Republican of Wisconsin, who voted against all the bills save two and abstained on one of those. In the House, we see the same situation. Representative Madden, Democrat of Indiana, voted favorably on all the bills. Representative Bennett, Republican of Michigan, voted favorably on only one of the bills, abstained on one, and voted against all the others. The records of the other Congressmen are spread out between these two extreme poles. The interesting thing is that the Congressmen's party affiliation seems to have had a great deal more to do with the way they voted on these bills than their Roman Catholic affiliation. Mr. O'Neill also cites a study made by Joseph L. Hansknecht, Jr., in a master's-degree thesis at the Catholic University of America in 1951.[3] Mr. Hansknecht's study analyzed the voting records of fifty Roman Catholic members of the House of Representatives in the Eighty-first Congress and compared them to a "comparable" group of non-Roman Catholic Congressmen's voting records. The thesis revealed that there was no identifiable "Catholic vote" in the House and once again indicated that Congressmen tended to vote as their party affiliation would indicate. This would throw considerable doubt on the reality of a "Catholic vote" among the citizenry generally—a matter to be discussed more fully in Chapter Eight.

How Bigotry Operates

One of the most dangerous things about religious bigotry is that it so often tends to use the same weapons which it suspects its foes of being ready to use. Some Protestants, firmly convinced that the day a Roman Catholic President is elected the Pope will move at least his summer quarters to this country, would gladly see the power of the State used to suppress the propagation of Roman Catholicism. The recent attempt of certain Protestant and secularist groups in California to remove the property-tax exemption from *all* nonprofit private schools was highly motivated by the fact that the Roman Church would have been most damaged by such a move. (The authors are happy to be able to report that their Episcopal Diocese was publicly active in the defeat of this measure.) To many Protestants the so-called "wall of separation between Church and State" is meant to be a large brick wall which can, from time to time, be dropped on the Roman Catholic Church. The Protestant bristles with anger at the Roman Church when that Church declares Protestantism to be a heresy; in the next breath he will be making equally serious judgments against the Roman Catholic.

The official Roman notion that "error has no right to exist" is heartily resented by the Protestants when they feel that this is aimed at their own existence. Yet the statements of many individual Protestants make it quite clear that they subscribe to precisely the same sentiments; the point of disagreement comes when they begin to define what is error. Many Protestants would gladly join in the suppression by almost any means of Roman Catholicism. These same Protestants are in the forefront of those who accuse the Roman Catholic Church of harboring a desire to use suppressive measures. It is the old theory of "preventive war." Many Protestants are so sure that the growth of the Roman Catholic Church represents a real threat to the American Constitution that they would gladly use unconstitutional means to control and suppress this growth. An analogy: one hesitates, the temper of the times being what it is, to point out that certain forms of "anti-Communism" can be a type of bigotry too. Yet so it is, as our remembrances of the days of the late Senator Joseph McCarthy will readily remind us. Just as McCarthyites were—and their successors are—quite willing to ignore our traditional liberties in order to overcome those whom they saw as a threat to our Constitution (by which they often meant their own political or economic views), so many Protestants are willing to do something similar in regard to what they see as the Roman Catholic threat.

Bigotry and "Anti-bigot" Bigotry

Does this mean that, since the existence of genuine anti-Roman Catholic bigotry is a fact, we should abhor any discussion of religious differences, even those which have a bearing on public concerns?

Of widespread application throughout the country is a sort of un-official code to this effect. It is quite evident in the mass media. One of us has had for five years a network program in the realm of religion and public affairs. Great latitude has been granted as to subject matter; but one of the two or three topics which has been definitely *verboten* is birth control. And although it is perfectly obvious that population control is a major world issue and one that bears on our nation's foreign policy, yet editorials in usually sensible newspapers have asserted that, because a religious difference is involved, this is not an issue before the public and that so to regard it is "bigotry." And this "code" applies in social conversation. One of the authors recalls from his Naval indoctrination course the instruction that in the officer's mess three subjects were to be avoided: "Women, politics, and religion" (which, incidentally, invited the query of one brash officer candidate, "What else will there be to talk about?").

Serious discussion about religion and its implications for man's personal and corporate life is as old as mankind itself. Why then the current "code" to the contrary? There are a number of reasons, but there is one very important factor which is particularly relevant here: the fear of being labeled a bigot. And this fear has been deliberately nourished by the popular press of the Roman Catholic Church. Methodists and Episcopalians can disagree—and publicly—and it is simply regarded as part of freedom in a pluralistic society. But let anyone conspicuously disagree with the Roman Catholic Church, even on a matter that vitally affects the rest of us, and to him will be immediately affixed the label BIGOT.

There are Roman Catholic publications, of limited circulation un-fortunately (because they are good magazines in general), which are by and large above this. Good examples are *America, Commonweal* and *Cross Currents*. But for publications with mass circulation, e.g., *Our Sunday Visitor*, and diocesan organs such as the Brooklyn *Tablet* and the Boston *Pilot*, often the formula is simply: disagreement= bigotry. And there is more than the attaching of this label. Though columns of type are used, all too often there is an unwillingness to discuss the given issue itself. Rather the space is used in *ad hominem* argument (ruled out as invalid by, incidentally, the great Catholic theologian, St. Thomas Aquinas). Refuge from real dialogue is taken in a smear or innuendo as to principal historic figures of the Communions to which the critics belong—and/or of the critics themselves.

A recent example will suffice to make the point. In response to the article in *Life* referred to in the Foreword, Mr. Dale Francis, the vivid columnist for *Our Sunday Visitor*, in the January 3, 1960 issue, expended 1400 words. None of these were devoted, as profitably as they might have been, to the two conflicting views within the Roman Catholic Church on Church-State relations (summarized in the *Life* article and fully discussed in Chapters Three, Four and Five). Space that could well have been used, for example, to support Fr. John Courtney Murray's attempt to develop a view compatible with American principles, was used instead for *ad hominem* remarks about the author. Mr. Francis's line: while Senator Kennedy was decorated for valiant Naval service, Bishop Pike left the Navy in 1944, a most crucial year (the Battle of Leyte is cited), for the ministry. This is totally false: the officer under discussion was honorably discharged, like everyone else, when the war was over and his services were no longer needed. (While serving his country full time he had studied—in off-duty hours —for ordination as a deacon; and—again in off-duty hours—assisted in a parish, and undertook his formal seminary training after the war.) The item had the effect which might have been expected: the clipping came to our attention through a letter from a Roman Catholic, referring to "a yellow streak." And a subsequent letter consisted of the word "Slacker," repeated thrice. But suppose that this fiction emerging from an ecclesiastical editorial office was actually true. What relevance did it have to the issue under discussion?

If writers of this type find, as to a particular live critic, no scrap of information which puts him in a bad light, then there is handy a stock set of retorts from "history": Henry VIII was a bad man and wanted a "divorce" (actually it was an annulment, familiar enough in Roman Catholic canon law and practice, then and now); Luther was too proud, ran off with a nun, etc., etc. Of course, this sort of thing makes the thoughtful and principled Roman Catholic thinkers of our day cringe.

Enlightening in this connection is a body of factual material which has come our way in recent weeks and which would make an interesting religio-sociological study in itself. Hundreds of letters have poured in on the foreign aid-birth control and Presidency issues. Eliminating brief complimentary notes, they fell into several well-defined categories: (1) a distinct minority, pro or con, dealing with one or another of the issues at stake; (2) a goodly number displaying bigotry against the Roman Catholic Church; and (3) a goodly number displaying what we have called "anti-bigot bigotry."

Typical of category (2): "Your *Life* article was much too friendly toward the Catholic Church. They are really plotting to take over." "You can't trust them." "They've fooled you, and you are their unwitting dupe." "There may seem to be liberal Catholics but they all take orders from the Pope." "The Papist bishops intend to control the country." "Eisenhower is a secret Catholic."

And in category (3) such sentiments as this: "What right do you have to disagree with what the one true Church teaches?" "What right have you to dress as a Bishop anyway?" (Many correspondents adopted "Mr. Pike" as the form of salutation.) "You're a fake!" "The devil is shining forth from your face" (referring to a rather adequate *Life* photo). "Do you think you can find God in your Church?" Plus numerous *ad hominem* comments and repeated references to "prejudice," "bigotry," and "un-American" *ad nauseam.*

The apposition of these two types of bigotry will remind the reader of other distressing antitheses all too familiar in American life: the white supremacist who automatically assumes that every Negro arrested must be guilty, the liberal who believes that every Negro arrested in the South has been "railroaded"; the "anti-Communist" who firmly believes that every person and organization investigated or "listed" by some Congressional committee or the Attorney-General (or who holds views to the left of President McKinley) is subversive, the "anti-anti-Communist" who believes that all such persons and groups are being "persecuted"; the conservative who automatically assumes that all strikes are based on unjust demands, the liberal who just as readily assumes that no picket line is to be crossed—"the union must have a just grievance or it wouldn't have struck."

Any such all out approach marks the end of any fruitful discussion of particular issues between persons holding differing positions—reasoned or irrational. It fractures the body politic. And, when Christians are involved, it keeps Christ's seamless robe rent.

But on the part of many "nice," "broad" people of various faiths—

and of none—there is great patience with Roman Catholic firmness and evident irritation with Protestant firmness. No newspaper editor or columnist, to our knowledge, criticized the Roman Catholic Bishops for their forthright Thanksgiving Day statement which brought birth control into the foreign policy (and, hence, political) realm. Nor would such criticism have been justified. But a good many—including some not of Roman persuasion—criticized those who stated an opposite view, even going so far as to say that we had "dragged religion into politics." But this is understandable. For so long Roman Catholics, by and large, were—economically and socially—an "underdog" minority (see Chapter Eight) that "nice" people still apply to them their natural reaction of defense of the "underdog." But times have changed: Roman Catholics are still a minority; but meanwhile they have become (happily, for anyone respecting the American ideal) a part of every level of our nation's life—social, economic, and political. They are not "underdogs" any longer, and they are entitled to receive the same respect—and criticism—that anyone else enjoys or endures. And now back to our main point: bigots among their number should be no more immune from back talk than bigots of any other background.

However, as between anti-Roman bigots and Roman Catholic bigots something can be said in the latter's favor. Their blind advocacy at least has a consistent theory behind it. Their Church has made a simple identification between itself and "the Truth." There can be no compromise with, or encouragement of, "heresy." There is only "one true Church"; the other churches are not part of the Church of Christ. Implicit—and often made explicit—is a very real contempt (or, at best, condescension) toward the Protestant "sects" (in which category all of us are lumped, whether an ancient Catholic Church like our own, or a venerable Reformation Church, or any sincere group of believers in Christ who may have first gathered together in His name). Granted this basic theological orientation, the otherwise quixotic semantics can be understood: a blatant attack, in a tract sold for a nickel in the narthex or in *Our Sunday Visitor*, in another Christian Communion is called "apologetics"; an analysis, no matter how objective, of a position of the Roman Catholic Church, or even a measured answer to the kind of attack just mentioned, is called "bigotry."

Those who understand the theological background of this apparently perverse type of verbalization really "take it" (even when we are on the receiving end of it) better than we accept the ignorant universalities hurled at the Roman Church by the other type of bigot. This explains why, though the senior author has never publicly attacked the Roman Catholic attitude, last year he took to pen, radio, and TV to rebut blanket attacks on the Roman Catholic Church spread throughout the state by many seeking support for the California initiative measure to tax parochial schools.

Yet we don't like bigotry from either direction, however justified or rationalized. And happily there are those within the Roman Catholic Church—still in the category of Elijah's "still, small voice"—who don't either. These, cleric and lay, are the leaven of the future. Completely loyal to the fundamental teachings of their Church, they seem able to maintain dialogue with some of the rest of us. And more than courtesy or good old American "fair play" is behind it: while they might grant the Roman thesis that error has no rights, they feel that erring people do—and anyway they are people. And some even grant that "heretics" have something to say to them and their Church (e.g., they will study—and admire—the Lutheran Kierkegaard or the Reformed Barth and Brunner). Such Roman Catholics are the leaven. And somewhat encouraging to them must have been the decision of warmhearted Pope John to change our liturgical appellation from "heretics" to "separated brethren."

Meanwhile, bigots are not the monopoly of either side. Nor are those who seek to give open—and precise—consideration to specific issues of importance to us as a people. Some of these issues, as far as the views or likely views of particular candidates go, are in fact related to religious differences. As to certain current problems of importance Roman Catholic teachings have a definite bearing. But theoretically —and practically, were the political configuration different—religious attitudes quite remote from the Roman Catholic Church, could have an equal significance. Looking at some such possibilities will help us keep this whole matter in perspective.

Legitimate Concerns

The Mennonite Church, a small but close-knit' sect, has a remarkable record of resistance to universal military training, having fled two different countries when such laws went into effect. This is admirable from an idealistic point of view, and the many Mennonites who served in conscientious objectors' camps during World War II are to be admired for their close adherence to the principles of their faith. However, it is unlikely that anyone from this background who was a loyal member of this group would—or should, as we see it—be chosen to be Secretary of Defense. For that matter, it is hard to imagine his taking part at any international conference table, it being well known by the various parties to the conference that in no wise could he approve of war or even defense. This is not a prejudiced statement against the Mennonites. Far from it: on the contrary, it is a simple recognition of what they have stood for through the years of their history and a recognition of the fact that any individual member of this church is likely to continue to stand for these things regardless of the office in which he may find himself. But, in any case, to ask the question would not be bigotry.

There is frequent recognition of this principle all over the country as jurors are disqualified in capital cases because they have religious objections to the death penalty. No prejudice is implied: there is merely a recognition of the fact that the death penalty is one of the possibilities in the case to be tried and that the matter of guilt must be decided by those open to imposing the penalties provided for by the law.

Christian Scientists are committed to a world view in which the material does not matter and in which only the spiritual has reality. We cannot agree with their theology; because we value our right so to disagree, we respect their right to hold this belief. However, this does not make a Christian Scientist a very likely prospect for the post of Secretary of Health, Education and Welfare in the President's cabinet. The person who fills this particular post must be a person who is thoroughly convinced, among other things, of the reality and the importance of the material order; a person who regarded disease as an illusion would not be a valuable person here. Thus, with no prejudice against Christian Science, we are able to say that there are some posts which Christian Scientists could not well fill. For similar reasons there are those who would not be enthusiastic about the appointment of either a thoroughgoing Zionist or an Arabophile who believes in the destruction of Israel as Assistant Secretary of State for Middle Eastern Affairs. We would defend the right of either to espouse his particular view and to seek to mold public opinion accordingly; but those who hold neither position would have every right to oppose such an appointment.

The Views of Candidates

In this spirit, we shall consider in the succeeding chapters certain views which Roman Catholics may well hold because of their Church allegiance. We are aware of the impossibility, as we have said, of saying that "all Roman Catholics" believe any single thing. There are, for instance, even as in Protestant Churches, many Roman Catholic laymen who are actually not interested enough in religion at all even to know what their Church's beliefs are, much less to care whether their personal working convictions are consistent with them. We shall, however, examine, in Chapters Three to Five, the particular doctrines of the Roman Catholic Church which seem to have bearing upon questions of a public nature and shall attempt to assay their possible weight with Roman Catholic candidates. Furthermore, in Chapters Six and Seven we shall examine particular political questions which do, in fact, have a religious grounding. We shall, in short, attempt to submerge bigotry by approaching the issues that really exist.

Whatever a President's views—whether religiously determined or not—there are, of course, Constitutional safeguards. There are thousands of things that the President of the United States cannot do, no matter how much he might wish to do them. Yet, despite the many safeguards, the executive branch of our government has a great deal of power. The power to veto, for instance, is an important one. While Congress can, of course, override a veto, it does not often do so. Even if it does, it takes time. Programs can be hampered by the use of the veto, even if not prevented altogether. There are many more subtle and unsubtle ways by which the President, who also has the power of appointment, can hamper or promote any given program. In the shaping in the President's mind of what is "good" and "bad" in legislation, in the rulings of administrative bodies, and even in the decisions of the courts (President Roosevelt did not hesitate to attempt to "pack" the court), his general religio-ethical framework is, of course, an important part of the motivation—sometimes consciously, sometimes unconsciously. As we will make clear later, we would not want it any other way. But, when the doctrines of any given Church have a relevance to important political questions, the voter has a right—indeed, a duty, insofar as he can inform himself—to adjudge whether the implications of these doctrines are likely to inform this or that policy of the candidate, if elected.

It is the contention of this book that, constitutional safeguards or no, these are real questions. This is not a question of bigotry but rather a question as to the real positions which the Roman Catholic Church takes and to which it expects its members to adhere. The basic question is: Are there any beliefs of the Roman Catholic Church that might impede the power of a President to fulfill his high office in accordance with American traditions?

A "Religious Test?"

To some readers this may seem as though we are moving in the direction of a "religious test" for public office. Such a step would, of course, be clearly unconstitutional. The religious test was one of the points of contention from which the Puritans were fleeing when they first came to our shores, and such tests have never been looked kindly upon within the United States. One can understand the occasion for the Test Acts in their historical context in, for instance, Great Britain. And Elizabeth I, whose subjects had been formally released from civil allegiance to her by Papal decree, may hardly be blamed if she was unwilling to see anyone appointed to public office until he had demonstrated his adherence to the Church of England. By the same token, the reluctance of Charles I to place any trust in adherents to the Puritan cause—who were against the King as well as against the Bishops—was well justified by his death upon the scaffold at the hands of those same Puritans. One can see the relevance, if not the justice, of a religious test under such conditions; but one can also rejoice that the framers of the American Constitution declared that no such religious test should ever obtain in the United States.

Over against this, however, is the fact that not only has no Roman Catholic ever been elected President of the United States but that, as recently as 1928, many spoke of "the unwritten law" which was supposed to indicate that none ever could be. We certainly have made it clear that we hold to no such "unwritten law" and indeed stand firmly against it.

The prohibition against a "religious test" is, as far as constitutional law is concerned, a prohibition against governmental action—whether executive, legislative, or judicial—not a prohibition against individual voters; and, as a matter of practical fact, there would be no way to adjudicate this realm of motivation. But we affirm that any decision to vote against a particular candidate simply because of his religious affiliation would definitely be an act of disloyalty to the spirit of American institutions. However, this does not by any means imply that citizens do not have the responsibility, in developing their judgment as to the proper selection among candidates, of weighing each significant issue which will affect the weal of our people—and of the world—insofar as this country's policies bear on the welfare of other peoples. And a given issue is not "blanked out" just because the different views toward it may in fact be geared to different religious convictions. To be so concerned is neither "bigotry" nor the imposition of a "religious test"; it is responsible citizenship.

CHAPTER TWO

Church and State

OBVIOUSLY, any discussion of the question of a Roman Catholic for the Presidency must revolve primarily about his views as to the relationship between Church and State. Some of those mentioned as candidates have already spoken out on this subject. It is to be assumed that any Roman Catholic candidate for the Presidency (or for the Vice-Presidency, for that matter) will sooner or later be placed in a position where he must make such a statement. In order for the voter properly to evaluate such a statement and to understand the context in which it will lie, it would be well for us at this point to spend some time in the discussion of the several possible views of this relationship. There are three main ones, which may be tagged (1) State over Church, (2) Church over State, and (3) God and Conscience over both.

State Over Church

This, of course, is the historic view which is generally referred to as "Erastianism." It became a possibility in Church-State relationships with the conversion of the Emperor Constantine to Christianity in 312 A.D. Ever since that time the Church has, from time to time in its history, been faced with this particular point of view. When we see this principle at work today, particularly in other countries, most of us, as Americans, readily reject the idea. We were appalled, for instance, at the attempt of Nazi Germany to rewrite the Old Testament in an attempt to eliminate its "Jewishness." By the same token we expressed great disapproval of such German churchmen as accepted the domination of the Nazi state over their churches—and, conversely, we felt a great admiration for Pastor Niemöller and others like him who stood firm against the demands of what we were convinced was a pagan state. We have been shocked at the attempts of the Communists in Russia to destroy the Holy Russian Orthodox Church and recently even more shocked by their apparently successful attempt, similar to that of the Czarist regime, to "use" the Church—with its teeth pulled. Such obvious policies, especially by states of which we disapprove, are always objectionable to the average American.

Even when practiced by nations which we generally approve, we neither understand nor really care for the State-over-Church position when it is called to our attention. The most ardent Anglophile among American Episcopalians still does not really feel comfortable with the thought of the appointment of Bishops of the Church of England by the Crown. Even if we have not thought through our personal positions on this matter we have a strong feeling that "something is wrong" when we see a Church expected to "take orders" from the State within whose bounds it exists. Two examples: the inability of our Church in England to revise its Prayer Book, because Parliament said "No" in 1928; and the concession that Pope Pius XI made in the Concordat with Mussolini, giving the government the right to object to the appointment of a given parish priest and also the right to appeal for his removal at any time "should grave reasons arise which render the continued presence of an ecclesiastic in a particular benefice undesirable."

And yet, despite our almost instinctive antipathy to the State-over-Church position when it is stated as such, many Americans unconsciously hold beliefs which reflect that view. In some cases we may hold these because it has never occurred to us to question them. One thinks, for instance, of the well-known case which took up the right of children who belong to a religious sect (Jehovah's Witnesses) which forbids salutes to the flag to be exempted from saluting the flag in the public schools.[1] The United States Supreme Court, to which the case was finally taken, overruled its own previous decision on the subject and affirmed the right of such children to be excused from this particular educational exercise. Yet many Americans, upon hearing of this decision, felt that this was "going too far" and that the children should be forced to display their patriotism in this particular way.

The experience of the churches in the State of California in regard to the "loyalty oath" which was imposed upon them is a case in point. Several years ago, at the height of the "security risk scare," a law was passed by the California legislature which required every Church which wished to take advantage of the property-tax exemption offered by the State to sign an oath stating that it did not advocate the overthrow of the American government. At no time during the period when the law was on the books did anyone seriously suggest that any church group was suspect of subversive activities. The fact remains, however, that the law, as written, was a clear case of the State exercising its authority over the Church and its appointment of clergy acting under a philosophical position which amounts to the State-over-Church position with which we are dealing here. The point of this illustration is that very few churches objected very strongly to this provision. Some of the churches signed it under protest—but they did sign it. On the other hand, there were churches which went out of their way to show their approval of such a law and at least one congregation publicly stated through its elected representatives that it felt the law to be a good thing. It may be that, had these people really understood the legal position they were taking, their action would have been different. However, the facts in the case seem to have been relatively clear-cut and there was actually amazingly little resistance to the loyalty oath itself. Fortunately, the law was later found to be unconstitutional as the result of action brought by a small number of congregations who were true to their principles and refused to sign the oath, thereby losing their tax exemption.

There are minor demonstrations of the State-over-Church position too. Most churches include an American flag as part of the décor of their chancel, and, in every case, the flag etiquette surrounding it is observed—that is to say, the American flag takes precedence, even within the church, over the church flag. This is, as we have said, a relatively minor example and yet it is a continual acting out in many of our congregations of the State-over-Church principle.

Finally, it is well known to every clergyman that many of his people feel that their country is their final allegiance and that, if they were ever forced to choose between their State and their Church, they would follow the State. The fact that they observe the feast days of Christian martyrs and that the latter grace the stained glass in the building and that, in most cases, these martyrs were brought to their deaths by standing up against an unfriendly State is apparently beside the point. The churches have very few potential martyrs today, and part of the reason for this is the wide acceptance of the view that the claim of the State is really superior to that of the Church.

The "Compartmental" View

There is another view which partakes of the nature of State over Church but which is not precisely that either. It is the view that a man's church affiliation is so far removed from the practicalities of political life that it need have no bearing upon his decisions in politics. This is the "watertight compartment" theory of religion and is held characteristically by the secularists, not to mention a great many Protestants, Jews, and Roman Catholics too. Actually, it is the view to which Al Smith was really appealing in his famous article in the *Atlantic Monthly* during the course of the 1928 campaign, and it is the view which Senator Kennedy has put forward during the early months of his campaign.

Governor Smith said:

> I summarize my creed as an American Catholic. I believe in the worship of God according to the faith and practice of the Roman Catholic Church. I recognize no power in the institutions of my Church to interfere with the operation of the Constitution of the United States or the enforcement of the law of the land. I believe in absolute freedom of conscience for all men and in equality of all churches, all sects, and all beliefs before the law as a matter of right and not as a matter of favor. I believe in the absolute separation of Church and State and the strict enforcement of the provisions of the Constitution that Congress shall make no law respecting an establishment of religion or prohibiting the free exercise thereof. I believe that no tribunal of any church has any power to make any decree of any force in the law of the land, other than to establish the status of its own communicants within its own church. I believe in the support of the public school as one of the cornerstones of American liberty. I believe in the right of every parent to choose whether his child shall be educated in the public school or in a religious school supported by those of his own faith. I believe in the principle of non-interference by this country in the internal affairs of other nations and that we should stand steadfastly against any such interference by whomsoever it may be urged and I believe in the common brotherhood of man under the common fatherhood of God.
>
> In this spirit I join with fellow Americans of all creeds in a fervent prayer that never again in this land will any public servant be challenged because of the faith in which he has tried to walk humbly with his God.[2]

Senator Kennedy, in an article appearing in *Look* magazine for March 3, 1959, said:

> Whatever one's religion in his private life may be, for the office-holder, nothing takes precedence over his oath to uphold the Constitution and all its parts—including the First Amendment and the strict separation of Church and State.
>
> Without reference to the Presidency, I believe as a Senator that the separation of Church and State is fundamental to our American concept and heritage and should remain so.
>
> I am flatly opposed to appointment of an Ambassador to the Vatican. Whatever advantages it might have in Rome—and I'm not convinced of these—they would be more than offset by the divisive effect at home.
>
> The First Amendment to the Constitution is an infinitely wise one. There can be no question of Federal funds being used for support of parochial or private schools. It's unconstitutional under the First Amendment as interpreted by the Supreme Court.
>
> I'm opposed to the Federal Government's extending support to sustain any church or its schools. As for such fringe matters as buses, lunches and other services, the issue is primarily social and economic and not religious. Each case must be judged on its merits within the law as interpreted by the courts.

This "compartmentalist" view says, in effect, that while Church and State both have their place, they have to do with entirely different areas of life. The Church in the eyes of the holder of this view is interested only in "otherworldly" or "spiritual" things. It is not a question of whether the State is over the Church or the Church is over the State, because the spheres of interest of the two institutions are so separate from each other that neither will have anything to say to the other in a man's political life. A man may be Protestant, Catholic, or Jewish; but one will not be able to deduce this from his behavior as an elected official. A man's official acts will not be affected in the least by the tenets of the religious faith to which he subscribes.

The national Catholic weekly review, *America*, in its issue for March 7, 1959, replied to Senator Kennedy's statement and said:

> We were somewhat taken aback, for instance, by the unvarnished statement that "whatever one's religion in his private life . . . nothing takes precedence over his oath. . . ." Mr. Kennedy doesn't really believe that. No religious man, be he Catholic, Protestant

or Jew, holds such an opinion. A man's conscience has a bearing on his public as well as his private life. As the St. Louis *Review* well expressed it: "When he implies that his religion, which teaches him to know, love and serve God above all things and to love his neighbor as himself, will not be allowed to interfere with his oath to the Constitution, it is the Constitution that ought to be examined, not his religion."[3]

In the issue of *The Commonweal* this New Year's Day, John Cogley says in his column that "a Catholic President . . . would have to acknowledge that the teachings of the Church are of prime importance to him." Strangely enough, Senator Kennedy's statement, far from posing the threat of ecclesiastical tyranny, would seem rather to represent the point of view of a thoroughgoing secularist, who really believes that a man's religion and his decision-making can be kept in two watertight compartments.

Politics and Religion

Any clergyman who has ever presumed to speak out on public questions has found his mail full of letters decrying the fact that he has "Brought religion into politics." This was the thesis of the bulk of some 1500 letters received by Dean Francis B. Sayre, Jr., of Washington Cathedral, and one of the present authors (then Dean of the Cathedral of St. John the Divine in New York City) when in 1954 they exchanged pulpits and, on a basis of religious and ethical principle, attacked "McCarthyism." What such people are really saying is that God should be confined to the sacristy or at the most to the realm of personal "do's and don'ts". Yet, inconsistently enough, such people are the first to applaud a sermon which seems to "use" God on some side they favor. For example, no clergyman of our acquaintance has been told that he unwarrantedly mixed politics and religion when he preached a sermon against Communism. Communism is a good thing to preach about, since it involves basic theological and ethical issues; but obviously a relevant sermon on it must get into the realm of politics, economics, and world affairs.

Whatever tradition within the Judaeo-Christian heritage a man espouses, one of the tenets of his faith is that God is the Lord of history, and that His concern is as broad as the whole weal of mankind—and this, of course, includes social, economic, and political arrangements, since "no man is an Iland intire of itself." Hence the

Church's concern must be this broad. Sometimes this involves speaking against the State: indeed, the "prophet" is here seen in one of his most characteristic roles.

For that matter, the so-called "American tradition" of the separation of Church and State contemplates that very possibility. The Church and State are to be forever separate, in order, among other reasons, that the Church may be free to exercise its prophetic function over against the State when necessary. It is only in states where Church and State are not separate that the Church is unable to criticize the State.

In America, at least, Christians have always felt free to speak out in the name of the Church against the State and against its policies. Far from having any feeling of "bringing religion into politics," the prophetic preacher acts upon the strong assurance that political behavior and decision-making are religious questions and that religious issues are continually being expressed in the political arena. As the editor of *Life* recently said editorially, "although our democracy . . . divorces Church and State, ours never contemplated a divorce between religion and society."[4]

No consistent Christian feels that there is this kind of separation; but secularists do, and it is secularism which fosters the idea. Even the secularist, however, when driven into a corner, will admit that a political official must be governed by his conscience when making decisions and, if he has thought about the question at all, he will realize that a man's conscience is largely molded by his religious beliefs. The very phrase "right or wrong" is meaningless unless a man has firm conviction as to what is right and what is wrong; and these convictions are almost certain to be drawn from the religious faith to which he adheres. Thus, to pretend that a man will not be guided in his political decisions by his religious faith is to suggest that he is a man who is willing to operate apart from his own conscience. The only thing worse than a President's making his decisions upon orders from his ecclesiastical superiors would be a President's making decisions apart from any religio-ethical code at all (which would mean he was following expediency alone); yet the suggestion of the "compartmentalists" is that this can be done. The suggestion is illogical; and yet a great many voters (not to mention a candidate or two) seem to feel that this is a sensible retort to those who want to "bring religion into politics." However a voter might react to a given candidate's position on an important matter, he has no right to resent the fact that that position happens to be grounded in the religious and/or philosophical outlook of the candidate, whatever it may be. A man's conscience is what it has become through exposure to religious beliefs—whether his own or those of the culture.

Church Over State

The second possible view is directly opposite to the one which we have been discussing. Since this view is not one which has ever been held officially by any of the several states of the Union, it is not one which has played a prominent part in our history. But it has played a part—generally unfortunate—in the history of other nations.

The most vivid illustration of this point of view, of course, will always be the picture of Henry IV kneeling in the snow at Canossa in 1077. Most historians consider this the "high-water mark" of the Papacy, when the Pope was able to make good his claim that he could uncrown emperors, and when one emperor, at least, acted as though he believed this to be so. It is interesting to note that this incident was also, from a negative point of view, the "high-water mark" in that after this the decline of the temporal power of the Papacy began, a decline which finally saw the Protestant Reformation and the establishment of independent Christian states.

But this Papal claim was not repudiated, as is illustrated by the attempt of Pope Pius V in 1570 to "uncrown" Queen Elizabeth I and to release her subjects from civil allegiance to her. The effect of this particular act, of course, was to demonstrate that more Englishmen were loyal to Elizabeth and the ancient Church of England than to the Pope. Another effect was to place those who did continue loyal to the Pope in an impossible position, since they were by definition "traitors" to the State and were forced to be disloyal either to their Church or to their nation.

Is This An Archaic Problem?

In terms of current problems this particular Church-State view may seem rather remote; but it has only been a few months since, in the implementation of a Papal decree, Sicilians were ordered by ecclesiastical authority not to support the Christian Social Union Party under penalty of excommunication. There is little doubt that this party was not a good one; but that is beside the point. The point is that even today Papal decrees are still implemented in this fashion, and this reflects "Church-over-State" thinking.

American Roman Catholics would doubtless point out that this could happen in Sicily but could not happen here. However, we must remember that one of the basic claims of the Roman Church is that it is "catholic" which, of course, means universal in its teaching and authority. Statements of the Roman Catholic authorities on this matter would tend to indicate that the Church at the present time will exercise such influence only in countries where it already has special prerogatives in the State. But then the really serious question arises, namely, "Is the Roman Church content to find itself in a nonpreferential status in any country?" In Chapter Three we deal with official statements which suggest that it is not but that its acceptance of a nonpreferential status is always a matter of expediency in terms of the country in which it finds itself. In short, the official position (but not the only one—see Chapter Four) would seem to be that the Church will grant equality to other religious views where it is forced to do so by the fact that it is a minority; but that, when it is numerically strong enough, it has a positive duty to begin to shape the State to suit its own ends.

Far from being a musty concept from a page in history, the Church-over-State theory of Church-State relationship is a twentieth-century reality. It is being carried out in countries where the Roman Church has the power to do so. It remains with many Roman Catholics an ideal, even for countries such as the United States, where the likelihood of its being actually put into practice is relatively remote.

God and Conscience Over Both Church and State

The third possible view on Church-State relationships is formed by what Paul Tillich has called "the Protestant principle." It affirms that only God is final and that all earthly institutions, ecclesiastical and civil, are *under judgment*. The Roman Catholic Church makes a simple identification between its visible institution and the "true Church." Not so Protestant churches; first of all virtually no one of them claims to be "the true church"; rather such a church conceives itself to be a part of the Church of Christ (albeit a "truer" part than others!); and in the view of such churches there is a remove between the visible churches and the true Church, the Kingdom of God.

The institution can express the meaning of the Kingdom—in varying degree in different times and places; but to the degree that he believes that it does not, the individual may feel called to express what he believes is God's judgment on the visible Church.

When Martin Luther, for instance, uttered his famous "Here I stand; I can do no other," he was not espousing either of the two previously discussed positions. Actually, he found himself at odds with both Church and State. The Holy Roman Empire was against him just as much as was the Papacy. At this point Martin Luther stood in the true prophetic tradition. He was opposed to both Church and State in the name of God and of his own individual conscience, which he felt was enlightened by the Holy Scriptures and the Holy Spirit.

The fact that Martin Luther's position changed radically so soon as he found a State which was willing to stand beside him is beside the point here. We are not attempting to make particular briefs for Martin Luther or for the Erastianism of much later German Lutheranism. The point that we would make is that at this historic moment Martin Luther stood as the spokesman for the "God-and-Conscience over Church-and-State" position.

That for a Roman Catholic it is not permitted to look in critical judgment at his Church in matters of conscience was typically asserted in *The Tidings*, official publication of the Archdiocese of Los Angeles (issue of August 15, 1958), as follows: "There is no conflict between the dictates of a Catholic's conscience and those of his Church, for the simple reason that the dictates of his conscience will always follow and reflect those of his Church . . . for its members' consciences are actually formed by the decrees of the Church."

Anyone who would agree with Dr. Tillich that only God is final and all earthly institutions are under judgment is unable to make the nation his highest allegiance. Bishop Berggrav in his resistance to the Nazi regime, Cardinal Mindszenty in his resistance to a Communist state, Bishop Reeves and Fr. Huddleston in their resistance to the apartheid policies of South Africa—all these are men whom we admire because of their willingness to put their consciences under God, ahead of any other demand. Actually, one of the primary purposes of the Bill of Rights of the American Constitution is precisely to protect this concept of the priority of conscience. What would be treason in some countries (in practically all of them at some point in their history) is a *privilege* built into our Constitution. In South Africa men are being tried for treason for publicly dissenting from government policy.

Dissent is in our best tradition, and the Bill of Rights is evidence that this is a nation founded on the principle that the claims of God and conscience can be a man's highest allegiance. In fact, the nation is safer with critical citizens, when their critique is grounded in an allegiance higher and more abiding than the nation itself.

Here we should notice the forms this judgment on the State takes. Even when the reformer seeks to bring God's judgment on the Church, he is not "a man from Mars": he speaks from within the Church and generally takes his presuppositions from the Church's heritage. And, when prophets speak against the State, time and time again in history, they have been speaking in the name of their Church, either as the appointed spokesman for a specific corporate declaration of the Church or as making explicit on the issue at stake the abiding moral teaching of his Church. In fact, often a given religious body exercises the prophetic function of the Church by a corporate action without an individual spokesman. Either way it occurs, in one sense this is "Church over State," but, actually, ultimately the spokesman or spokesmen are following "God and Conscience over State," as is illustrated by the fact that on occasion, where the Church itself has "missed the point" or has been cowed by State authority or popular opinion, prophets speak out on religious and ethical grounds nevertheless. But the Constitutional right so to speak out is in no way diminished by the fact that there happens to be—as there usually is—a concurrence between the prophetic statement and the official position of the Church. But this does not mean that "built in" to our national allegiance is the freedom—either of an individual or of a religious body—to give to another entity a higher priority than that given to one's nation, whether this entity be nation or Church—or a combination of both, as in the case of the Vatican.

These are the variant views on the Church-State relationship. Many people may hold variations of these views, but all such views would fall under one or the other of these heads. The important question is: To which of these views does the Roman Catholic Church subscribe? This is not an easy question to answer because within the Roman Catholic Church are spokesmen for two contrary positions. The first two views (State over Church, Church over State) in their pure form both require beliefs which are contrary to the American Constitution. The third view (God and Conscience over both) is that which is "built into" our Constitution. In the next three chapters we shall discuss the conflicting statements regarding these views which issue from the Roman Catholic Church.

CHAPTER THREE

The Official View of the Roman Catholic Church

THE "OFFICIAL VIEW" of the Roman Catholic Church as to Church-State relations is not without a venerable genealogy. In 1075 A.D. Pope Gregory VII (Hildebrand) made a broad claim: He declared that he had the right to depose and to remove Emperors. More than that, he demonstrated it a few years later by threatening Henry IV, declaring that, as the occupants of the See of Rome could "bind and loose in heaven so also they could take away and grant kingdoms, principalities and all other possessions of man, according to man's merit."[1] His priorities are clear: the relationship of the Pope to a head of State was "as the sun to the moon." In 1302, Pope Boniface VIII in his famous bull, *Unam sanctum*, declared that it was "necessary to salvation to believe that every human creature was subject to the Roman Pontiff." For him there were two swords (and they were literally carried in front of him in his official processions), the spiritual and the temporal. Boniface declared: ". . . The latter, indeed, must be exercised for the Church, the former by the Church. The former [by the hand] of the priest, the latter by the hand of kings and soldiers, but at the will and sufferance of the priest. For it is necessary that a sword be under a sword, and that temporal authority be subject to spiritual power." He further boasted that he could depose a king as he would discharge a groom.

Space will not permit us to trace the development of this point of view step by step to modern times; but the nineteenth century is rich in such pronouncements. Pope Gregory XVI in the encyclical, *Mirari vos* (1832), condemned liberty of conscience, as well as freedom of thought, freedom of speech, freedom of the press, and separation of Church and State. At the same time, a personal letter was sent by Cardinal Pacca in the Vatican to the French political thinker Lamennais making specific to Lamennais's teachings the application of this encyclical. The letter said, "[your doctrines] on the liberty of worship and the liberty of the press . . . are equally reprehensible in the extreme and in opposition to the teaching, the maxims, and the practice of the Church. They have astonished and dismayed the Holy Father very much, for, if in certain circumstances, prudence compels their toleration as a lesser evil, such doctrines can never be presented by a Catholic as good or desirable."[2]

Let us now move to the remarkable *Syllabus of Errors,* promulgated by Pius IX in 1864, and its accompanying encyclical *Quanta cura.* The following notions, taken for granted as true in this country, were solemnly declared to be errors:

> The Church has not the power of using force, nor has she any temporal power, direct or indirect.
>
> National Churches, withdrawn from the authority of the Roman pontiff and altogether separated [e.g., The Church of England and the Lutheran Churches in the Scandanavian countries] can be established.
>
> In the case of conflicting laws enacted by the two powers, the civil law prevails.
>
> The entire government of public schools in which the youth of a Christian state is educated . . . may and ought to appertain to the civil power, and belong to it so far that no other authority whatsoever should be recognized as having any right to interfere in the discipline of the schools, the arrangement of the studies, conferring of degrees, and the choice or approval of the teachers.
>
> The best theory of civil society requires the popular schools open to children of every class of the people, and generally all public institutes who attend to the instruction in letters and philosophical sciences and for carrying on the education of youth, to be free from all ecclesiastical authority, control and interference. . . .
>
> Every man is free to embrace and profess that religion which, guided by the light of reason, he shall consider true.
>
> The Church ought to be separated from the State and the State from the Church.

At this point we should interrupt to remind you that the statements here being listed are not affirmations of acceptable principles (though they sound like that), but a listing of principles which are to be con-

demned and which are not to be accepted by any Roman Catholic.
Now we go on to four more "errors":

> In the present day it is no longer expedient that the Catholic
> religion should be held as the only religion of the State, to the
> exclusion of all other forms of worship.
>
> Hence, it has been wisely decided by law in some Catholic
> countries, that persons coming to reside therein shall enjoy the
> public exercise of their own peculiar worship.
>
> Moreover, it is false that the civil liberty of every form of worship,
> and the full power, given to all, of overtly and publicly manifesting
> any opinions whatsoever and thoughts, conduce more easily to cor-
> rupt the morals and minds of the people, and to propagate the pest
> of indifferentism.
>
> It is lawful to refuse obedience to legitimate princes, and even
> to rebel against them [rather hard on the Boston Tea Party!].

The accompanying encyclical solemnly declares that it is contrary to
"the teachings of the Holy Scriptures, of the Church, and of the Holy
Fathers" to assert that "the best condition of human society is that
wherein no duty is recognized by the Government of correcting by
enacted penalties, the violators of the Catholic Religion, except when
the maintenance of the public peace requires it." The Pope condemned those who hold the "totally false notion," indeed "the in-
sanity," of the view "that the liberty of conscience and of worship is
the peculiar or inalienable [shades of the Declaration of Independ-
ence] right of every man, which should be proclaimed by law [as in
the American Bill of Rights]. . . ."

Is This Still Authoritative?

Granted, all this was said about a century ago. Can we not forget it?
In the case of almost any other church, we could. But in the Roman
Catholic Church, as we shall see in Chapter Five, ex cathedra decrees
of Popes are regarded as eternally infallible, and his other decrees are
at the least entitled, as a matter of discipline, to "internal assent." But,
in any case, Roman Catholic authorities have ever since taken the
same general line. To move up a couple of decades, Pope Leo XIII
declared in his encyclical *Libertas* that the idea of separation of
Church from State is a "fatal principle." *Immortale Dei* in 1885 specifically condemned the State which "believes that it is not obliged to
make public profession of any religion; or to inquire which of the very

many religions is the only one true; or to prefer one religion to all the rest; or show any form of religion special favor; but, on the contrary, is bound to grant equal rights to every creed. . . ." In almost the same breath he condemns the theory "that everyone is to be free to follow whatever religion he prefers, or none at all if he disapprove of all." He went on to say that the temporal power of the Church was "the surest safeguard" of the Church's vital independence.

> . . . the *civil* wisdom of private persons seems to consist entirely in the loyal execution of the precepts of lawful authority . . . the faithful should accept religiously that their rule of conduct, the political wisdom of ecclesiastical authority . . . subjects are warned that they shall not arrogantly judge the life of their superiors; even should it be their lot to see such superiors acting blameworthily . . . should such superiors really have committed blamable actions, their inferiors, and full of the fear of God must not judge them, even in the mental blame, except in a perpetual spirit of respect and submission. The actions of superiors are not to be touched by the sword of speech, even when they seem to deserve a righteous rebuke [our italics].

To move to the turn of the century, we find the Vatican publication *Osservatore Romano* declaring that "as the Pope is the sovereign of the Church, he is also the sovereign of every other society and of every other kingdom."

What Do American Roman Catholics Believe?

But do any Catholics in this country believe such things? Definitely. The late Rt. Rev. John A. Ryan, of the Catholic University of America and formerly Director of the Department of Social Action of the National Catholic Welfare Conference, and the Rev. Dr. Francis J. Boland, C.S.C., of the University of Notre Dame, in their *Catholic Principles of Politics,* issued under Cardinal Spellman's imprimatur, take this position:

> Quite distinct from the performance of false religious worship and preaching to the members of the erring sect, is the propagation of the false doctrine among Catholics. This could become a source of injury, a positive menace, to the religious welfare of true believers. Against such an evil they have a right of protection by the Catholic State.[3]

The authors realize that what they label as "superficial champions of religious liberty" will promptly and indignantly denounce the foregoing propositions as the essence of intolerance. They answer:

> They are intolerant, but not therefore unreasonable. Error has not the same rights as truth. Since the profession and practice of error are contrary to human welfare, how can error have rights? How can the voluntary toleration of error be justified?[4]

Next they deal with "the objection that the foregoing argument can be turned against Catholics by a non-Catholic State." This they meet by two replies:

> First, if such a State should prohibit Catholic worship or preaching on the plea that it was wrong and injurious to the community, the assumption would be false; therefore, the two cases are not parallel. Second, a Protestant State could not logically take such an attitude (although many of them did so in former centuries) because no Protestant sect claims to be infallible.[5]

To be fair to the authors, they do not anticipate the immediate realization of a sufficient Roman Catholic pre-eminence in this country to make their principles locally applicable. But they like to dream of the ideal State. For example:

> Suppose that the constitutional obstacle to proscription of non-Catholics has been legitimately removed and they themselves have become numerically insignificant; what then would be the proper course of action for a Catholic State? Apparently, the latter State could logically tolerate only such religious activities as were confined to the members of the dissenting group. It could not permit them to carry on general propaganda nor accord their organization certain privileges that had formerly been extended to all religious corporations, for example, exemption from taxation.[6]

And why? Their answer is at least direct:

> If there is only one true religion, and if its possession is the most important good in life for States as well as individuals, then the public profession, protection, and promotion of this religion and the legal prohibition of all direct assaults upon it, must become one of the most obvious and fundamental duties of the State. For it is the business of the State to safeguard and promote human welfare in all departments of life.[7]

Monsignor Ryan and Fr. Boland are sensitive enough to realize that such a position might well disturb non-Roman Catholic Americans. But their retort is, "Nevertheless, we can not yield up the principles of eternal and unchangeable truth in order to avoid the enmity of such unreasonable persons. Moreover, it would be a futile policy; for they would not think us sincere."[8]

Another American theologian who had been saying such things for some time, and continued to do so thereafter, was honored with the deanery of the most distinguished intellectual font of religious learning in the American Roman Catholic Church, namely, the School of Sacred Theology of the Catholic University of America. The Very Rev. Francis J. Connell said in 1949:

> I do not assert that the State has the right to repress religious error merely because it is error; I believe that the State has the right of repression and limitation (although often it is not expedient to use it) when error is doing harm to the spiritual interests of the Catholic citizens.[9]

In *The Jurist*, writing in 1953, Fr. Connell clarified his position further:

> However much we may praise [the American system], as far as our land is concerned, it is not *per se* preferable to the system in which the one true Church would be acknowledged and specially favored.[10]

Then he proceeds to quote the Papal brief *Longinqua oceani* addressed to the Bishops of the United States on January 6, 1895, by Leo XIII:

> The Church among you is hampered by no legal bonds, is protected against violence by common law and just judgments, and receives the opportunity to live and to act without being mistreated. But, although all this is true, it would be erroneous to conclude that from America is to be sought the example of the best condition of the Church, or that it is universally lawful and expedient for civil and religious matters to be dissociated, as in America. That Catholicism is in a good condition among you, and is even enjoying a prosperous growth, is by all means to be ascribed to the fecundity with which the Church is divinely endowed, in virtue of which, unless men or circumstances interfere, the Church spontaneously

expands and spreads; but she would bring forth much more abundant fruits if, in addition to the liberty, she enjoyed the favor of the law and the patronage of public authority.

From this, Fr. Connell concludes:

> We must not, therefore, regard the American system as the best, absolutely speaking, even though we may justly praise the liberty which the Church enjoys in our land. Above all, we may not condemn the system of concord and cooperation between Church and State which *Christ willed* to be the proper situation when circumstances permit—that is, in a land where Catholicism is the religion of practically all the people and there exists a long-standing Catholic tradition. *Neither should we object, at least as far as principles are involved, to the restrictions which Catholic nations of our own day are placing on non-Catholic propaganda* [italics ours].[11]

Last June Fr. Connell's institution bestowed a Doctor of Laws degree on the Roman prelate most "avid" these days in proclaiming special and exclusive rights of the Roman Catholic Church in regard to the State. He is Alfredo Cardinal Ottaviani, the head, under the Pope, of the Vatican's Holy Office. He is, perhaps, the most representative figure in the Roman Catholic Church, save the Pope himself. (He was the one recently widely pictured, receiving for the Pope the new American Cardinals-elect.) He maintains that the traditional teaching of his Church on Church-State relations are of permanent authority and are not to be dismissed as relating only to specific historical situations.[12] For him, the Church's continuous position on this matter is not a pragmatic one, to meet certain crucial situations, but has its basis in Revelation and in the declarations of the Popes: "These principles," he says, "are solid and unchangeable: they were valid in the time of Innocent III and Boniface VIII; but they are also valid in the time of Leo XIII and Pius XII who confirms them in more than one document."[13]

Cardinal Ottaviani is quite clear that not all religions have the same right before the civil law. He is all for the fundamental rights of man and particularly religious rights—but only for those who hold the truth. There are those of us who are in error (which presumably would include the authors of this book) whom he would not regard as having the same claim. He feels that Divine Law, justice, and reason would be violated by the notion that every religion should have indifferently the same treatment and rights. More than that he feels that such a view would lead to atheism. He is quite aware of the fact that in the United States there are "dissident brethren" who are unhappy with a number of "Catholic States" who suppress Protestant activity. But he regards such complainants as "imitating the Communist ardor."[14]

In 1953 the *New York Times* reported that it had ascertained from the Vatican that "the views expressed by Cardinal Ottaviani were unexceptionable and orthodox."[15]

Further American Authorities

In an article in *American Ecclesiastical Review* in 1950, the Very Rev. Msgr. George W. Shea takes note of what we shall later call the "American Interpretation," but points out that the traditional Catholic doctrine on Church and State (as per Cardinal Ottaviani) is still the authoritative view of the Church, and makes use of Leo XIII's *Immortale Dei* to bolster that position. Fr. Shea said, "As I see it, these various papal pronouncements bear upon the state, *qua* state. . . . The State, to which man's God-given social nature impels him, is a creature of God, and as such is bound by the natural law to worship God and in the way he wills. If this be conceded, it should not be necessary to pursue any further the significance of such papal utterances for the various points. . . ."[16]

Msgr. Shea also quotes Canon 1381, of the Code of Canon Law to show that the Church has the authority and right to supervise the teaching of religion in public schools and in all schools, and that this Canon would also imply that the Church is right to require the state to repress heresy and error from such teachings. He said, "As I see it, Canon 1381, §3, amounts to the assertion by the Church of her right to call upon the civil authorities who control the public schools, to inhibit the spread of heresy. Moreover, the Church has called upon various states to acknowledge this her right, as could readily be shown from various modern Concordats." He goes on to conclude that the State has the right and, when called upon to exercise it, the duty of "repressing heresy."

In a series of articles in 1953 and 1954 in the *American Ecclesiastical Review*, Msgr. Joseph C. Fenton of the Catholic University of America also takes note of those who would liberalize the official views on the Church-State relationship. Fr. Fenton says:

A mere glance at the theological articles on the Church and State which have appeared over the course of the last few years . . . will suffice to show very clearly that there is nothing like any unanimity among American theologians in favor of the "liberal view." As a matter of fact, those who oppose this view would seem to outnumber those who favor it. At any rate, it is evidently untrue to state or to imply that American theologians as a group have taken a national stand on a purely theological question.[17]

Speaking of Cardinal Ottaviani's "official view," as over against the so-called "American interpretation," Msgr. Fenton declared:

Those who would like to believe, and to have others believe, that authoritative pontifical teaching on this and other subjects has changed or developed in such a way that some things presented as true by Popes like Pius IX and Leo XIII have been completely, or partially, denied by more recent pontiffs, would not like what [Cardinal Ottaviani] had to say on this subject.[18]

It is clear that, for Msgr. Fenton, at least, the "official" view is still the only valid one.

Further Word from Abroad

Even blunter is the Jesuit world organ, *Civiltà Cattolica:* "The Roman Catholic Church, convinced through its divine prerogatives of being the only true Church, must demand the right of freedom for herself alone, because such a right can only be possessed by truth, never by error. As to other religions, the Church will certainly never draw the sword [comforting thought!], but she will require that by legitimate means they shall not be allowed to propagate false doctrine." The article grants that in countries like the United States, "Catholics will be obliged to ask full religious freedom for all, resigned to being forced to cohabit where they alone should rightfully be allowed to live."[19]

Apart from the Popes themselves one of the most explicit statements of the official position was made by an English prelate from whose fine translation of the Bible so many of us have profited. The Rt. Rev. Msgr. Ronald Knox has given the following analysis in *The Belief of Catholics* (published with the imprimatur of the Archdiocese of the Roman Catholic Primate in England):

Is it just, since thought is free, to penalise *in any way* differences of speculative outlook? Ought not every Church, however powerful, to act as a body corporate within the State, exercising no form of coercion except that of exclusion from its own spiritual privileges? It is very plain that this has not been the Catholic theory in times past. There has been, in Catholic nations, a definite alliance between the secular and the spiritual power. So, to be sure, has there been among Protestant nations. But may it be understood that in our enlightened age Catholics would repudiate the notion of any such alliance in future?

It must be freely admitted that this is not so. You cannot bind over the Catholic Church, as the price of your adhesion to her doctrines, to waive all right of invoking the secular arm in defence of her own principles. The circumstances in which such a possibility could be realised are indeed sufficiently remote. You have to assume, for practical purposes, a country with a very strong Catholic majority, the overwhelming body of the nation. Probably (though not certainly) you would have to assume that the non-Catholic minority are innovators, newly in revolt against the Catholic system, with no ancestral traditions, no vested interests to be respected. Given such circumstances, is it certain that the Catholic Government of the nation would have no right to insist on the Catholic religion being taught in all schools open to the general public, and even to deport or imprison those who unsettled the minds of its subjects with new doctrines?

It is certain that the Church would claim that right for the Catholic Government, even if considerations of prudence forbade its exercise in fact. The Catholic Church will not be one amongst the philosophies. Her children believe, not that her doctrines may be true, but that they *are* true, and consequently part of the normal make up of a man's mind; not even a parent can legitimately refuse such education to his child. They recognise, however, that such truths (unlike the mathematical axioms) can be argued against; that simple minds can easily be seduced by the sophistries of plausible error; they recognise, further, that the divorce between speculative belief and practical conduct is a divorce in thought, not in fact; that the unchecked developments of false theories result in ethical aberrations—Anabaptism yesterday, Bolshevism to-day—which are a menace even to the social order.

Such considerations would reasonably be invoked if a body of Catholic patriots, entrusted with the government of a Catholic State, should deny to the innovator the right of spreading his doctrines publicly, and so endangering the domination of Catholic principles among their fellow countrymen.

It is frequently argued that if Catholics have at the back of their system such notions of "toleration," it is unreasonable in them to complain when a modern State restricts, in its turn, the political or educational liberty which they themselves wish to enjoy. What is sauce for the goose is sauce, surely, for the gander. The contention is ill-conceived. For, when we demand liberty in the modern State, we are appealing to its own principles, not to ours.[20]

In the first edition of his work (published in 1927), Msgr. Knox put the matter even more strongly.[21] There the last sentence of the second paragraph quoted above read: "Given such circumstances, is it certain that the Catholic Government of the nation would have no right to insist on Catholic education being universal (which is a form of coercion), and even to deport or imprison those who unsettled the minds of its subjects with new doctrines?" The second sentence of the third paragraph quoted above read: "And for those reasons a body of Catholic patriots, entrusted with the Government of a Catholic State, will not shrink even from repressive measures in order to perpetuate the secure domination of Catholic principles among their fellow-countrymen." In the Preface to the new edition, Msgr. Knox indicates that the changes in the later edition were "not by way of withdrawing anything I have said . . . in 1927."

It was just seven years ago that the Pope took a similar position. The late Pius XII declared that "what is not in accord with the truth and with the moral norm has objectively no right to existence, propagation or action," and reaffirmed the fact that the Church "in principle cannot approve complete separation" between Church and State.[22]

We have not heard from Pope John XXIII in such broad terms. Having been in office a very short time, he has been content to take a dim view of only one of the customarily accepted freedoms, namely the freedom of the press. He urged "legal limitations"; and a boycott by Roman Catholics. This does not augur well for hope that he might reverse his predecessors in their position on our other customary liberties.

But a quite different view of this whole matter has been expressed within the Roman Catholic Church.

CHAPTER FOUR

An American Interpretation

IF THE PRECEDENTS quoted in the last chapter were the only "line" which had been taken within the Roman Catholic Church on the subject at hand, there would be no reason to write further. The only conclusion that any loyal American could draw would be simply that it would be dangerous and entirely unfitting for any member of a Church proclaiming such views to become our Chief Executive. But other Roman Catholic spokesmen have taken quite a different line, and, although no one of them is of the rank of Pope, their points of view should be studied carefully before any conclusions are drawn.

For convenience, we are calling this alternative point of view "an American interpretation." We use the adjective fully aware of the fact that "Americanism" (the general spirit of adaptation of Roman Catholic teaching to the American scene symbolized by the figure of Fr. Isaac Hecker, founder of the Paulist Fathers), was condemned by Pope Leo XIII, to the disappointment of the great Cardinal Gibbons. But this is not determinative; there are those within as well as without the Roman Catholic Church who feel that the Pope did not really understand what Fr. Hecker was trying to say. The fact is that ten years after the Papal brief *Testem benevolentiae*, by which this condemnation was uttered, Cardinal Gibbons asserted that Roman Catholics in this country "prefer its American form of government before any other . . . they accept the Constitution without reserve, with no desire as Catholics to see it changed in any feature. They can, with a clear conscience, swear to uphold it."[1]

Cardinal Gibbons's Position

Cardinal Gibbons did grant that the union of Church and State "is ideally best." But he added, "history assuredly does not prove that it is always practically best. There is a union that is inimical to the interests of religion, and consequently to the State . . . there is a separation that is for the best interests of both . . . In our country, separation is a necessity; and it is a separation that works best in the interests of religion—as Mr. Taft [the President] recently stated—as well as for the good of the State."[2]

Some may be unhappy that this great American figure conceded so readily that union of his Church and State is the ideal; nevertheless, they should grant that his statement was courageous in the face of the plain statements of the Popes. Nor should we overlook Cardinal Gibbons's firm view that the Pope will be transgressing the law he is bound to defend if he interferes in "purely civil" matters. He asserted that the consciences of the members of his Church would force them to resist any such interference.

Another great figure of the same period, Archbishop John Ireland of Milwaukee, went even further. He said:

> . . . The Church is at home under all forms of government. The one condition of the legitimacy of a form of government, in the eyes of the Church, is that it be accepted by the people. The Church has never said that she prefers one form of government above another. But, so far as I may from my own thoughts interpret the principles of the Church, I say that the government of the people, by the people, and for the people is, more than any other, the polity under which the Catholic Church, the church of the people, breathes air most congenial to her mind and heart.[3]

Archbishop Ireland was confident that it was necessary to put "neither Church before Country, nor Country before Church." In his view, "Church and Country work together in altogether different spheres. The Church is supreme in one order of things; the State is supreme in another order."[4] This is a far cry from Pope Boniface VIII's "two swords." In fact, it is almost a statement of the "watertight compartment" view analyzed in Chapter Two, held by many American citizens today, and most recently asserted by Senator Kennedy.

John Courtney Murray

While I am sure that he shares the same love for American institutions with the prelates just quoted, the Rev. John Courtney Murray, S.J., one of the most distinguished theologians (of any faith) in our time, is more articulate in expressing the fact of the apparent conflict between allegiance of such liberal Democratic ideas and allegiance to the traditional view of his Church. In recent years he has written extensively on this subject. Since he has developed, more fully than anyone, a position consonant not only with American ideals but with what is consciously or unconsciously the point of view of the average American Roman Catholic, we do not hesitate to quote at length one of his many important passages on this subject:

> Concretely the present problem concerns the provisions guaranteeing "the free exercise of religion." That has become characteristic of the Democratic state constitution. At least, this is usually conceived to be the major aspect of the problem. In fuller form, the problem may be stated as follows: Can the Church accept, as a valid adaptation of principle to the legitimate idea of democratic government and to the historically developed idea of "the people" (to which the democratic government appeals for its legitimacy), a constitutional system of Church-State relations with these three characteristics: (1) the freedom of the Church is guaranteed in a guarantee to the people of the free exercise of religion; (2) the harmony of law and social institutions with the demands of the Christian conscience is to be effected by the people themselves through the medium of free political institutions and freedom of association; (3) the cooperation between Church and State takes these three forms: (a) constitutional protection of the freedom of the Church and all her institutional activities; (b) the effort of the State to perform its own function of justice, social welfare, and the favoring within society of those conditions of order and freedom necessary for human development; (c) the effort of the Church, through the action of a laity conscious of its Christian and civic responsibilities, to effect that Christianization of society in all its dimensions which will enable and oblige the State, as the instrument of society, to function in a Christian sense.
>
> This lengthy question is not to be transformed into a brief tendentious one: can the Church at last come to terms with Continental Liberalism? The answer to that nineteenth-century question is still a nineteenth-century answer: No. But, when the nineteenth-

century question has been given its nineteenth-century answer, the twentieth-century question still remains unanswered. To it, as put, I am inclined to answer in the affirmative. The Church can, if she wishes, permit her principles of freedom, harmony, and cooperation thus to be applied to the political reality of the democratic state. The application of each of the three principles (freedom, harmony, cooperation) can be justified in terms of traditional Catholic thought, political and theological.

The resulting system would not, indeed, be some "ideal" realization of Church-State relations, some sort of "new thesis." The point is that no "ideal" realizations are possible in history; no application of principle can claim to be a "thesis".[5]

Separation Can Be Supported

Fr. Murray insists that the traditional American position in the separation of Church and State can be supported within Roman Catholic dogma. He is quite aware of the apparently contrary position of Pope Pius IX. But he avers that all of this was directed against a particular evil of a particular time, i.e., nineteenth-century European liberalism. There was a threat in the anticlerical spirit to the established rights of the Church. He sees American democracy in quite a different light. Therefore, he is able to draw the conclusion that the Papal defense of the State-Church principle "does not represent a permanent and unalterable exigence of Catholic principles." He feels that "the Church can, if she will . . . consent to other institutionalizations of Church-State relationships and regard them as *aequo jure* valid, vital and necessary adaptations of principle to legitimate political and social developments."[6]

Fr. Murray has pushed to the fore certain primary principles which he believes are more fundamental than the particular position taken by the Popes in response to Continental liberalism or than the appropriate response to American democracy. These are, as indicated above, the freedom of the Church, necessary harmony between the State and the conscience of its citizens, and the necessary co-operation of Church and State. He asserts that "the permanent purpose of the Church in relation to the State is to maintain her doctrine of juridical and social dualism under the primacy of the spiritual, against the tendency to juridical and social monism under the primacy of the political."[7] When he refers to the primacy of the spiritual, he makes clear "this primacy does not imply that the temporal power is some-how instrumental to the proper *ends* of the spiritual power or the Christian people. Nor does it have, per se, connotations of an ecclesi-astical jurisdiction over the temporal. Primacy, per se, asserts a superior dignity. It also asserts influence, whose manner of exercise will be "in accord with the kind of dignity and superiority asserted." He adds, "this is the principle; beyond this all else is in the realm of application of principle to institutionalized forms of influence."[8]

By influence, he does not mean a direct claim, by concordat or otherwise, upon the official government of a State. Rather, he means the legitimate influence of "the Christian people" upon the decisions of government. Obviously, the guide to the objectives of this influence would be, for Fr. Murray, the visible Roman Catholic Church. But he does not go further and exclude from freedom within the State those outside that Church.

A "Catholic State?"

Fr. Murray is bold enough to debunk the concept of the "Catholic State" which is so prominent in the analysis of those supporting the "official view." Naturally, he recognizes that there is a Catholic Church and that there are Catholic individuals. But whatever the civil set-up, there cannot be a Catholic State. The officials of a State, as individuals seeking to apply the fruits of their consciences in whatever ways the State permits their influence, may be Catholic. But a State is not "Catholic," no matter what the counting of noses indicates in regard to percentages of population.[9] Whether or not his Church may have judged—or have adjudged—this to be sound doctrine, it would certainly seem to be sound political theory.

In short, Fr. Murray believes that the Roman Catholic Church can be persuaded to acknowledge American principles. The issue for him is clear:

Is the Church in America to be allowed to travel her own historical pattern and forward her own particular solutions to the Church-State problems, remaining faithful to essential Catholic principles and to the specific character of the political tradition within which her institutional life has been lived? Or, on the other hand, is the Church in America to repudiate the history of America and what is most unique about it—its installation of a political tradition sharply in contrast to that of modern continental Europe?[10]

This is a good question. It should be the question in every voter's mind, should a Roman Catholic run for President or Vice-President.

Support for Fr. Murray

Fr. Murray is hardly without modern support. In 1948, the same year that Rome's *Civiltà Cattolica* was being firm about "truth" and "error," the American Roman Catholic Bishops issued the following statement:

> We feel with deep conviction that for the sake of both good citizenship and religion there should be a reaffirmation of our original American tradition of free cooperation between government and religious bodies—cooperation involving no special privilege to any group and no restriction on the religious liberty of any citizen. We solemnly disclaim any intent or desire to alter this prudent and fair American policy of government in dealing with the delicate problems that have their source in the divided religious allegiance of our citizens. We call upon our Catholic people to seek in their faith an inspiration and a guide in making an informed contribution to good citizenship.[11]

And in the same vein the late Archbishop John T. McNicholas, speaking as chairman of the Administrative Board of the National Catholic Welfare Conference in 1948:

> We deny absolutely and without any qualification that the Catholic Bishops in the United States are seeking a union of Church and State by any endeavors whatsoever, either proximate or remote. If tomorrow Catholics constitute a majority in our country, they would not seek a union of Church and State. They would then, as now, uphold the Constitution and all its Amendments, recognizing the moral obligation imposed on all Catholics to observe and defend the Constitution and its Amendments.[12]

These statements are a refreshing change from the rather ominous declaration in the Pastoral Letter of Roman Catholic Bishops and Archbishops of the United States in the Third Plenary Council in Baltimore in 1884:

> It is obvious in countries like the United States where from rudimentary beginnings our organization is only gradually advancing toward perfection, the full application of these laws is impracticable; but in proportion as they become practicable, it is our desire, not less than the Holy See, that they should go into effect.

Commonweal, Roman Catholic journal of opinion, takes a strong editorial stand in favor of the "American Interpretation":

> The classic position on the Catholic state may once have been opposite and suitable to a sacral civilization, and it is, indeed, still orthodox and logical as a textbook position. But it seems to many in Leo's words, out of date, and useless, and even harmful if applied in the twentieth century—and this is whether it be applied in the United States or Spain. Cardinal Ottaviani, himself recognized at least the possibility of this when, in his address, he admitted that the application of the "intransigent stand" he was enunciating in principle might have to be tempered by such social—as distinct from religious concepts—as the rights of man, even in an overwhelmingly Catholic state.
>
> . . . Since there seems no possibility of any "Catholic State" existing, either now or in the future, in which a rigid application of the abstract position enunciated by Cardinal Ottaviani would not be tragically unwise, discussion of this position must remain rather academic. Taken out of the academy . . . it is a discussion which may do real harm by arousing fear and misunderstanding of the Church.[13]

The general position which we have called the "American Interpretation" also has some support on the Continent, as witnessed by the position taken by the Belgian Dominican, Fr. Augustan Leonard. Writing in *Cross Currents*, Fr. Leonard takes an "existential" view of the question of religious liberty and toleration for those outside the Church or "in error." He says:

> The very nature of faith—even more precisely its liberty—must furnish us with the principles for adopting the Christian manner of life to a society which is no longer coextensive with the visible Church. . . . Constructive toleration is certainly not the suit of religious indifference: it depends far more on the reverence which the Catholic Church pays to divine truth. . . . The principle of religious liberty, when in operation on the civil plane, does not constitute in any way a denial of the rights of God or of the universal and absolute value of the two faiths. To insist that the state is obliged to leave the citizen free to obey his conscience within the limits of the natural law and the common good, is not to state philosophically that he possesses complete freedom to acknowledge or reject God. Religious liberty is defined not in relation to God but

in relation to a civil institution which has no title to intervene in a religious domain beyond the competence of civil government.[14]

In assessing the reason for the lack of acceptance of the "social encyclicals" of Leo XIII and Pius XI, the Italian, Conrad Bonacina, also writing in *Cross Currents*, goes even further than Fr. Murray. He remarks:

> In principle . . . the Catholic Church is of no political color. She numbers in her communion people of almost every shade of political opinion and no one has the right to say of this or that shade that it is any more Catholic than any other.[15]

He here seems to imply that it may be possible even for the Pope to exceed his "rights" in dealing with certain types of subject matter in official pronouncements.

Support for the American interpretation and the recognition that it seems to conflict with the "official" view has recently been given by a leading Roman Catholic layman, Senator Eugene J. McCarthy of Minnesota. In an interview in *The New Republic*[16] he stated in discussing the *Civiltà Cattolica* statement: "It is obvious . . . that there are some Catholics who hold that point of view. However, this is not the viewpoint which is held by all Catholics." He added: "I cannot, of course, foretell what might happen if the majority of the citizens of the United States were to be Catholic. The Constitution would still be a strong defense of individual liberties. It is my opinion, however, that a majority of the Catholics in the United States today—a strong majority—would support the position of the Bishops [quoted earlier]."

In all fairness we would add that Senator McCarthy's view is doubtless the one held—consciously or unconsciously—by most of his fellow churchmen in this country.

And yet this conclusion runs directly counter to one of the strictures in the *Syllabus of Errors*: among the "errors" which the Pope solemnly condemns is the position that "the children of the Christian and Catholic Church are divided among themselves" about this issue!

CHAPTER FIVE

Some Difficulties

THE "AMERICAN INTERPRETATION" sounds fine. It would seem that any Roman Catholic candidate could easily qualify by simply saying, "That's where I stand," (or, as in the case of Governor Smith or of Senator Kennedy, by actually affirming a position further to the "ecclesiastical left"). In fact, most Americans are well tutored in any circles to mouth a "regardless of race, color, or creed" at the drop of a hat. It's rather what you expect an American to say; it is rather gauche to intimate anything to the contrary or even to qualify it. It is under the actual pressure of decision-making that the basic teachings of one's religious affiliation come out. Therefore, it is appropriate that we consider the degree to which this more palatable view is tenable with abiding Roman Catholic theology, polity, and practice.

The fact is that, though the "American interpretation" is apparently desirable from the point of view of most Americans, there are, it would appear, three difficulties for Roman Catholics:

1. It hardly jibes with the actual practice of the Roman Catholic Church in a number of countries in which its adherents constitute—or appear to constitute—the considerable majority.

2. Even its most outstanding theologian-exponent does not plead for it as finally right, but rather as a permissible view within Roman Catholicism.

3. It would seem to run straight up against the doctrine of Papal infallibility.

Practice Elsewhere Versus the "American Interpretation"
All the while that the Roman Catholic Bishops have been asserting

their loyalty to American pluralism and freedom and that Fr. Murray has been developing his fine series of articles in *Theological Studies* and that outstanding laymen, like the late Governor Smith and Senator Kennedy, have been affirming their allegiance to American principles, the fact is that Protestants have been having a very rough time in Spain, in Italy, and in a number of Latin American countries, and we have seen no protest as to these persecutions and restrictions on the part of the Roman Catholic papers of wide circulation; in fact, there has been a persistent protest against the protesters.

A usual answer given in the United States is that these restrictions are the fault of the State, not of the Church. But it is fairly evident that the latter is behind the State restrictions. In fact, from time to time, archbishops and primates issue cries of alarm about even the limited freedom of Protestants in these lands and even go so far as to chide—and sometimes censure—the officials of the State for their laxity.

The American Roman Catholic defense may go one step further and say that the statement of local archbishops and primates is not necessarily the position of the Roman Catholic Church. But it is to be noted that the Vatican has issued no open and clear rebuke to the high ecclesiastics taking this position, and the Vatican is quite capable of acting when a local cleric gets out of line (e.g., its prompt support of archdiocesan authority against Fr. Leonard Feeney of Boston when he insisted on a greater degree of exclusiveness for the Roman Catholic Church as a means of salvation than the church itself was prepared to maintain) or in support of the local episcopate on issues within a given nation (e.g., the rather quick response of Pope John in regard to the foreign aid-birth control issue). The silence of the Vatican in regard to the ecclesiastics' statements against religious freedom for Protestants in certain Latin countries therefore speaks volumes.

One need not repeat here what everyone has read in the newspapers: the difficulties of the Union Protestant seminary in Madrid; the barring of clerical attire to non-Romans; the banning of "Protestant" Bibles; the requirement that in the case of Protestant churches, no evidences of an ecclesiastical edifice protrude on the scene; delays and frequent refusals to allow the opening of new Protestant churches or the building of churches for congregations long in existence, grave difficulties put in the way of the marriage of persons who are converts from Roman Catholicism to other Christian positions, *et ad infinitum*.

Also no news to any reader are the limitations in Italy on various Protestant groups (though there has been for some decades a considerable tolerance of churches that are more "standard brand" and have a longer genealogy, e.g., Waldensian, Anglican, Presbyterian, etc.). The press has regularly reported the dire consequences (though perhaps in recent months somewhat less dire) involved in trying to be a Protestant in Colombia.

As to the latter type of persecutions, Roman Catholics sometimes add a further argument: this is neither the fault of the Church nor of the State; it is simply the undirected action of mobs. But those making this defense overlook the evidence in a number of cases of direction of the action of mobs by clerics and the conspicuous absence of rebukes to the mobs on the part of clergy, who are presumably committed to the furtherance of Christian charity.

Moreover, in any rejoinders on this subject there is frequent reference to "proselytizing" and "propaganda." One does not have to be too semantically sophisticated to realize that these are "color words": it is proselytizing when someone is being converted from you to something else; it is evangelism if someone of a different tradition is being converted to your church!

If it be said that this is all simply human nature and that no group is very much interested in the alienation of the civil rights of other groups, one can answer that this is, indeed, human nature, but a pretty unredeemed human nature, and there are evidences from time to time that human nature can be salvaged in this regard. Note, for example, the strong concern of Jewish groups (e.g., the American Jewish Congress, the American Jewish Committee, and B'nai B'rith) for the civil rights of Negroes. And it is with some pride that we recall that the Episcopal Diocese of New York took an active part in a movement to end the appointment of juvenile probation officers in New York City on a "religious test"; specifically on the basis of the percentage breakdown of offenders—a basis which resulted in very few Jewish appointees and produced a relatively inordinate number of appointees of other faiths. More than that, our Church took a stand against the Manual of the New York Board of Education on "moral and spiritual values" which would have required a "religious test" of atheist or agnostic school teachers; since the latter had no "institutional" defender, the Diocese decided to serve as their champion, in terms of American principles. In short, such things can happen.

What Roman Catholic newspapers of wide circulation have gone out of their way to defend the Protestants in Colombia, in Spain, in Italy? The question is particularly poignant because of the universal character of the claims of a "catholic Church." If, since Roman Catholic professions of loyalty to the principles of religious freedom are presumably genuine, then why no concern as to whether these principles have application anywhere else? These same Church papers are very fearful that we might recognize Red China, a country condemnable because it does not permit the freedoms to which we are accustomed in this country; but indicate no dissent from similar policies in Roman Catholic dominated Latin countries.

There may be a fuller answer to all of this than has yet been given: but it casts some doubt on the viability of "the American interpretation" within the Roman Catholic Church.

The Intrinsic Ambivalence in the "American Interpretation"

It should be readily granted that spokesmen like Fr. Murray do not buy the idea, so current among Roman Catholics, that Spain is the "model" Catholic state. He says:

> The issue is whether the Spanish constitutional concept of "the religion of the state" and all its present operative consequences, is actually that inherent exigence of Catholic *faith* which Spanish apologists maintain it to be. Does Spain, in point of principle, represent "the ideal Catholic regime?"[1]

He grants that the question is doctrinal but in answering the question he says, "But were I to give an answer, it would be, of course, 'No.'"

On the other hand, in pressing his position within the Roman Catholic Church (and for this, from our point of view, all praise!), there is a real ambivalence between the result to be achieved and the point of view from which it is sought to be achieved. He maintains that the "permanent purpose of the Church in her relationship with the State, is to maintain her doctrine of juridical and social dualism under the primacy of the spiritual, against the tendency to juridical and social monism under the primacy of the political." We have in Chapter Two supported precisely the same sentiment. However, for those who accept the Protestant principle, "the primacy of the spiritual" is a judgment on both Church and State, whereas for a Roman Catholic it would generally appear that his Church is finally determinative as to spiritual matters, since for the Roman Catholic there is a simple identification between the visible Church and the Kingdom of God. Hence, in the last analysis, Church is still over State. The Roman Catholic may say, and quite sincerely, that with regard to these possible conflicts his conscience will be his guide; but it is his Church which is the ultimate mentor of his conscience. It, in fact, turned out this way with regard to Senator Kennedy's reaction to the matter of the foreign aid-birth control issue for nations who desire this help. When pressed by James Reston of the *New York Times,* he finally did concede that it would be unwise to deny this aid to countries requesting it, but twenty-four hours later in Denver he had "gotten in line" and made a flat statement against the granting of such aid under any circumstances. He had said that the fact that the Bishops of his Church had spoken had no bearing on his decision, but twenty-four hours later he landed not only in Denver but precisely on the Bishops' airstrip. All this may have been purely coincidental, or it may be that the teaching of his Church as to the awful sinfulness of birth control in the end regulated his conscience with regard to the morality of the whole matter.

On the other hand, another Roman Catholic aspirant, Governor Brown, was quite willing to take an "independent line" on this matter and say that he would not want to deny such aid to a country desiring it. We like Governor Brown's view better; but it would seem that Senator Kennedy's was, in fact, more loyal to his Church, a Church which leaves no room for "the Protestant principle" of judgment by the individual on views of the Church on moral questions.

Now Fr. Murray goes on to argue that "the first principle is that of freedom of the Church"[2]—by which, of course, he means his own Church. But most of us would say that the first principle here is the freedom of *all* churches. For him the second principle is that of necessary harmony between the "two laws." It is quite evident that what he really means here is that the State must provide the appropriate harmonies for the melody played by the Church (note: not "the churches"). Finally, Fr. Murray affords us an expression of hope that it is permissible within the Roman Catholic fold to hold a view in line with religious freedom for non-Roman Catholics. His sincere endorsement of the separation of Church and State becomes a mere hope that the Church will "consent to other institutionalizations and regard them as *aequo jure* valid, vital and a necessary adaptation of principle for legitimate political and social developments." Crucial here is the little Latin phrase, which means "with equal right." He would seem to claim no innate superiority for the American system of pluralistic freedom; he simply expresses the hope that it may be allowed an equal standing within the Church alongside of the "official view." One would gather from the whole tenor of his writings that he personally would rather have written *"majore jure"* or even *"solo jure."* It is perfectly evident that he doesn't like, at least in terms of any universal application, the view of the Popes and of Cardinal Ottaviani; but *aequo jure* was probably as far as he could go in this statement. In other words, even Fr. Murray does not raise the question as to whether there is room in the Roman Catholic scheme for the views of Pope Pius XII or Cardinal Ottaviani; he is really only raising the question as to whether there is room within the Church for *his* view, i.e., the view in accord with generally understood American principles. (But let not these queries be regarded as a criticism of Fr. Murray. It is easy for, e.g., a Baptist, not under any central authority and in a tradition which even refuses Federal grants for the construction of hospitals, to speak openly for American principles; it takes much more courage for a sincere American Roman Catholic theologian like Fr. Murray to go as far as he has in his published and oral comments.)

The Effect on Infallibility

The second difficulty leads us to a third: the most basic one. Is the doctrine of the infallibility of the Pope a roadblock to the "American interpretation?" To restate the question, is it logically possible for an American Roman Catholic to hold a view on these vital matters of Church-State relations which is contrary to the announced word of the Popes? It is obviously factually possible. Fr. Murray is a priest and Jesuit in good standing still; and as to Senator Kennedy, he has publicly dissociated his religious convictions from his political decision-making—a radical view, not only as Roman Catholic dogma goes but even as to the prevailing doctrine of any responsible church within the Judaeo-Christian tradition—and, yet, no Bull of Excommunication has been issued. Therefore, some will ask at this point what difference logic makes.

In the long run, it does make a difference. From our pastoral experience we have run into mixed marriages where the couple had covertly agreed in advance that promises signed in regard to the raising of children as Roman Catholics would not, in fact, be implemented, and yet where later on, after a baby was born, the Roman Catholic party insisted upon the fulfillment of the plain words of the signed agreement (often because of pressure from Roman Catholic grandparents, supported by clergy). At what point a Roman Catholic President might have impressed upon him the logic of his commitments to his Church no one can ascertain in advance. In the first place, the President's spiritual adviser might well find it within his province to point out that this or that specific policy was not in line with "infallible" Roman Catholic teaching; and, in any case, the Roman Catholic press could be counted upon to call any such lapses to his attention. Finally, the Roman Catholic citizens would much more expect a Roman Catholic to adhere to their Church's teaching than they would a Protestant. It could well be that a man's good intentions would not be strong enough to withstand such factors as these, and regardless of the degree to which this feeling was articulated by this portion of our citizenry, it would represent a pressure on the President —especially on one with an eye to maximum support for re-election.

But a way out has been suggested by a distinguished Jesuit scholar. In the December 12, 1959, issue of *America*, the Rev. John R. Connery, S.J., professor of moral theology at West Baden College, discusses the question of the President's responsibility on an issue where the infallible teaching authority of the Church has already declared itself, as would arise in the case of foreign aid toward birth control. He said:

> . . . It is one thing for a person to condemn and disapprove of wrongdoing, and quite another for him to dissociate himself from it . . . I merely wish to point out that cooperating with wrongdoing does not necessarily involve personal commitment to the evil . . . It would be wrong for a Catholic President to initiate a birth control program. But it is not so easy to determine what his moral obligation would be if he were called upon to cooperate with a birth control program initiated by others . . . if [he] were presented with a bill sponsoring a birth control program . . . It would clearly be wrong for him to approve the program, and I am inclined to think . . . that signing the bill would be tantamount to such approval. However, the Constitution itself seems to offer a third alternative, a way in which the President can dissociate himself from a bill without vetoing it.[3]

Here he refers to Article 1, §7, of the Constitution, which allows a bill not returned by the President within ten days to become a law as though he had signed it.

Whether or not such a calculated abnegation of moral responsibility in the face of something which one is under obligation to regard as evil may be so simply countenanced within the Roman Catholic ethic, we do not know. Suffice it to say that Fr. Connery's analysis would certainly not be permissible within the ethical teachings of the rest of the Judaeo-Christian tradition—which, put simply, requires us to seek to achieve the will of God both by positive and negative action. But, quite apart from all this, an action in accordance with Fr. Connery's proposal would satisfy neither Roman Catholics nor the rest of the citizenry. As for the former, if Congress or the ICA developed a plan for such American assistance to a country requesting it, those loyal to the Roman Catholic position that all this is a grave moral evil would most certainly expect a Roman Catholic President to quash the whole business with the fullest authority at his command. On the other hand, those who believe such assistance to be a positive moral good, both in the interests of the United States and for the welfare of countries in a desperate situation, would most certainly expect more from their President than that he simply sit by and hope that it wouldn't happen; they would want from him positive leadership in the promotion of such a program, and, if need be, influential effort in getting it through Congress or seeing that it was developed by the ICA. In short, on an issue of this gravity, there is no room for a fence sitter.

Thus, there is no way around the effect on a Roman Catholic President of the "infallible" declarations of his Church. Some of the problems are already apparent and are discussed in this book. But we can never know when a new "infallible" declaration may be made and what bearing it may have upon issues important to the nation. We should not be so parochial in the United States as to assume that every Papal utterance will be timed in terms of American interests or the peculiar position of Roman Catholic Presidents. The fundamental problem is, of course, the attitude toward Church-State relations. Should the present Pope or a future one decide really to "lay it on the line" and reaffirm the "official view," as previous Popes have continuously done, where then would a Roman Catholic President stand? What we mean is this: should there be a new Papal declaration that the official Papal view (and the only Papal view to date) shall be the *exclusive view*, and that the view of sincere Americans like Fr. Murray is heretical, then Fr. Murray and the Roman Catholic President would have a difficult choice: either (1) to conform to the anti-American view in their teaching and practice, or (2) to reject Papal infallibility—which for sincere men (the kind, presumably, we are talking about) would mean leaving the Roman Catholic Church.

Or, let's put the question another way. Can the Pope really accept the "American interpretation" and not by so doing contradict the doctrine of Infallibility? An editorial in *Life* magazine expresses with all good will the hope that "Rome itself might conceivably some day endorse" the "American interpretation."[4] With equal good will, this would be the hope of many of us. But, the problem is: having once committed itself to the Doctrine of Infallibility, can this Church so function?

This would have been no problem in, e.g., 1850. As of that time, the Pope had not been declared infallible. In fact, the Irish catechism in use at that time declared that it was not part of the teaching of the Roman Catholic Church—and never would be. As the English Prime Minister, William Gladstone, recalled in his *Vatican Decrees and Their Bearing on Civil Allegiance*, during the Parliamentary discussions in the eighteenth and nineteenth centuries of the release of Roman Catholics in England and Ireland from their civil disabilities, Roman Catholic Bishops, priests, and laymen gave solemn assurances of their rejection of Infallibility.[5] The Irish Bishops went so far as to assert that it was known throughout the whole Roman Catholic Church that this doctrine could not be made an article of faith. As a matter of fact, at the 1870 Vatican Council, which defined the dogma of Infallibility, there were a good many present, including a majority of the American Bishops, who either did not believe in that doctrine or thought that its declaration was exceedingly "untimely"; and such views were held by distinguished intellectual leaders in the Church such as John Henry Newman and Lord Acton. Nevertheless, the dogma passed, many of those opposed to it having left the Council to avoid voting against their consciences.

Before 1870, the problem would have been easier. A Council or later Pope at any point could say that as to declarations in favor of the "official view," the previous Popes were simply wrong. This approach would be quite in line with the action the Church took in judging as heretics Popes Vigilius and Honorius (Pope Vigilius was condemned in 553 by the Fifth Ecumenical Council, at Constantinople, and Pope Honorius was anathematized in 681 by the Sixth Ecumenical Council, also at Constantinople—for formal heretical declarations in the realm of Christology).

Things before 1870 would have been just as they are with the Anglican Church today. In 1920 the Lambeth Conference declared contraception sinful; in 1948 it gave a very limited assent, in terms of an exception to a rule. But in 1958 we laid upon the consciences of our people a positive responsibility for family planning. And the General Assembly of the Presbyterian Church (now the United Presbyterian Church) changed its mind on this matter between 1930 and last year. But once a Pope has officially declared himself in a matter of this type it is not as easy for a successor to reverse his stand as it might have been before 1870. For in that year the Pope was declared infallible when he speaks *ex cathedra* in matters of faith and morals—and what he declared is *irreformable* by the Church. This latter assertion was, incidentally, contrary to the whole posture of the early fifteenth-century Councils of Pisa and Florence.

Some may say Pius IX issued the *Syllabus of Errors* before the Infallibility decree of 1870; hence, it need not be regarded as infallible. But, obviously, the infallibility doctrine, to be tenable at all, must be regarded as retroactive and has been so interpreted ever since. The Roman Catholic Church does not claim that the Papacy for the first time in 1870 became infallible; the claim is that in 1870 it was officially ascertained that the Bishop of the See of Rome had always been infallible.

The Pope whose status was in question during the deliberations of the Vatican Council to which he was host had not wanted any limitations placed on his infallibility; nevertheless, throughout the deliberations and debates a limitation was placed. The words of the decree:

> . . . The Roman Pontiff, when he speaks *ex cathedra*, that is, when, in discharge of the office of pastor and teacher of all Christians, by virtue of his supreme Apostolic authority, he defines a doctrine regarding faith or morals to be held by the universal Church, is, by the divine assistance promised to him in Blessed Peter, possessed of that infallibility with which the divine Redeemer

willed that His Church should be endowed in defining doctrine regarding faith or morals; and that, therefore, such definitions of the Roman pontiff are of themselves, and not from the consent of the Church, irreformable.

What Does "Ex Cathedra" Mean?

There is not agreement within the Roman Catholic Church as to the number of the actual "*ex cathedra*" declarations. For example, a number of Roman Catholic theologians and other clergy on the Continent treat Anglican orders as valid on the ground that the Papal bull to the contrary (*Apostolicae curae*, 1896) dealt with a matter of history and not of faith and morals. It was doubtless because of this lack of agreement that the late Pope, in issuing the encyclical *Humani generis* sought to "build in" a declaration as to the infallible character of the utterance.

. . . What is expounded in the encyclicals of the Roman pontiffs concerning the nature and the constitution of the Church is habitually and deliberately set aside by some with the intent of substituting certain vague notions which they pretend to have found in the ancient fathers, especially the Greeks. The Popes, they claim, do not wish to pass judgment on what are matters of dispute among theologians; so recourse must be had to the primitive sources, and the latter constitutions and decrees of the magisterium must be interpreted in accordance with the writings of antiquity. While this may sound clever, it is really a sophism. It is true that as a rule the Popes leave theologians free in those matters on which the respectable authorities hold divergent opinions; but as history teaches, many points that were formerly open to dispute, are so no longer. Nor must it be thought that what is contained in encyclical letters does not of itself demand assent, on the pretext that the Popes do not exercise in them the supreme power of their teaching authority. Rather, such teachings belong to the ordinary magisterium, of which it is true to say: "He who heareth you heareth me"; very often, too, what is expounded and inculcated in the encyclical letters, already appertains to true Catholic doctrine for other reasons. But if the the supreme pontiffs in their official documents purposely pass judgment on a matter debated until then, it is obvious to all that the matter, according to the mind and will of the same pontiffs cannot be considered any longer a question open for discussion among theologians.

The encyclical *Quanta cura* and its appended *Syllabus of Errors* has no such built-in validation; but what is said above by Pius XII would apply with full force, since *Quanta cura* is no less an encyclical than *Humani generis*. In fact the Jesuit weekly, *America* (issue of April 30, 1927), has cited Pius IX's encyclical and syllabus as an example of an encyclical which "contains teaching set forth on the infallible authority of the Holy See."

It cannot be questioned that the subject matter falls within the category of "faith and morals." Certainly a Church which honors St. Augustine of Hippo, whose major works dealt with the *civitas Dei* and the *civitas terrestris* would not exclude the relationship of "the two societies" from the realm of doctrine. Nor could anyone deny the relationship of this question to ethics and morals, unless he would limit ethics to purely personal one-to-one relationships and would exclude from morals the public political life of man—a view which, to its credit, has not been characteristic of the Roman Catholic Church.

The only possible "but" in this regard would lie in the other aspect of the *ex cathedra* limitation, as defined in the decree of the Vatican Council: ". . . when, in discharge of the office of pastor and doctor of all Christians . . . he defines a doctrine . . . to be held by the universal Church. . . ." As we have indicated above, Fr. Murray regards the *Syllabus* as speaking primarily to a type of secularism and anticlericalism typified by the new democracies arising in Europe at the period. It can certainly be readily agreed that the situation presented by these new political developments represented the *occasion* of the issuance of the *Syllabus*. On the other hand, a study of the document itself (and the prior Papal declarations which it cites), will show that the definition of virtually all the "errors" was in universal form. And this, even though the United States (where there were by this time a considerable number of Roman Catholics) represented a type of democracy which Fr. Murray avers is quite different from those on the Continent then agitating the Pope. Yet there were no qualifying phrases, no indications of exceptions to the principles being laid down—and it is hard to believe that the Bishop of Rome had never heard of the English and the American democratic systems.

Thus it is not surprising that there are Roman Catholic authorities who adjudge the *Syllabus* as infallible. And among those who are not entirely sure that it is, there are authorities who nevertheless regard it as binding on all Roman Catholics, both as to exterior conformity and "interior assent."

The following is the position of the *Catholic Encyclopedia:*

> The findings of the Syllabus of Pius IX is typically explained by Catholic theologians. All are of the opinion that many of the propositions are condemned, if not in the Syllabus, then certainly in other final decisions of the infallible teaching authority of the Church, for instance in the encyclical *Quanta cura.* There is no agreement, however, on the question of whether each thesis condemned in the Syllabus is infallibly false, merely because it is condemned in the Syllabus. Many theologians are of the opinion that Syllabus as such an infallible teaching authority is to be ascribed, whether due to an ex cathedra decision of the Pope or to the subsequent acceptance by the Church. Others question this. So long as Rome has not decided the question, everyone is free to follow the opinion he chooses. Even should the condemnation of many propositions have that unchangeableness peculiar to infallible decisions, nevertheless the binding force of the condemnation in regard to all the propositions is beyond doubt. For the Syllabus, as appears from the official communication of Cardinal Antonelli, is a decision given by the Pope speaking as universal teacher and judge to Catholics the world over. All Catholics, therefore, are bound to accept the Syllabus. Exteriorly, they may neither in word nor in writing oppose its content; they must also assent to it interiorly.[6]

This view would seem to be given additional weight by the following quotation from the 1885 encyclical, "The Catholic Constitution of States":

> In the difficult course of events, Catholic believers, if they will give heed to us as it behooves them to do, will readily see what are the duties of each as much in the opinions which they ought to hold as in the things which they ought to do. In the matter of thinking, it is necessary for them to embrace and firmly hold all that the Roman Pontiffs have transmitted to them as often as circumstances make necessary. Especially and particularly with reference to what are called "modern liberties", which are so greatly coveted in these days, they must abide by the Judgment of the Apostolic See, and each believer is bound to believe thereupon what the Holy See Itself thinks.

The same pontiff, in his 1890 encyclical, "The Chief Duties of Catholic Citizens," said further:

In defining the limits of the obedience owed to the pastors of souls, but most of all to the authority of the Roman Pontiff, it must not be supposed that it is only to be yielded in relation to the dogmas of which the obstinate denial cannot be disjoined from the crime of heresy. Nay, further, it is not enough sincerely and firmly to assent to doctrines which, though not defined by any solemn pronouncement of the Church, are by her proposed to belief as divinely revealed in her common and universal teaching, and which the Vatican Council declared are to be believed with Catholic and divine faith. But this likewise must be reckoned amongst the duties of Christians, that they allow themselves to be ruled and directed by the authority and leadership of bishops, and, above all, of the Apostolic See.

Msgr. Joseph Fenton, of the faculty of theology of the Catholic University of America, affirms in the *American Ecclesiastical Review*:

It is quite probable that some of the teachings set forth on the authority of the various papal encyclicals are infallible statements of the Holy Father. It is absolutely certain that all the teachings contained in these documents and dependent upon their authority merit at least an internal religious assent from every Catholic.[7]

The Jesuit weekly, *America* (issue of April 30, 1957), has taken a strong position on the authority of encyclicals:

A papal encyclical invariably demands from Catholics, first, respect in view of the source from which it emanates; and next, absolute obedience . . . Hence, the genuine Roman Catholic at once yields respect and obedience.[8]

And the standard treatise on the Canon Law of the Roman Catholic Church, Pezzani's *Codex Sanctae Ecclesiae Romanae* states:

Even in the matter of opinions, which concern neither dogma nor morals, it is a strict obligation to receive and to profess, the case occurring of past, present, and future instructions and directions of the sovereign pontiffs. And it is not enough to yield them external obedience in silence and respect. The only worthy and religious obedience is inward, the obedience of the heart.

To return to the effect of infallibility on the Church-State issue, some accustomed to the Protestant ethos might say, "Why can't a man like Fr. Murray settle the argument and say that while the Pope is generally infallible, on *this* question the Pope was simply wrong?" The difficulty is that when it comes to infallibility you can't miss even once. As Aristotle and St. Thomas Aquinas have wisely said, a negative particular disproves an affirmative universal. If, as it would appear on this question, the Pope was speaking *ex cathedra*, then to say that on a given point a particular Pope was wrong, is to say that the doctrine of Infallibility is fallacious. But even if *Quanta cura* and the *Syllabus* are not "infallible" because not *ex cathedra*, there still remains the stricture of external conformity and interior assent.

We hope that there is some way round this dilemma. The "American interpretation" is much more compatible with the religious views of the rest of us, let alone the general philosophy of American Constitutional life. But, if this "way round" is available, then we should hope for some firm declaration from the Pope, in effect telling the chief of his Holy Office, Cardinal Ottaviani, that his position is wrong and that certain American spokesmen are right. The argument set forth in Roman Catholic pamphlets and books for the appropriateness of Infallibility is that by this means definite answers can be given the Church and the world on important questions. Moreover, with a sharp division within the Roman Catholic Church itself (a division in this country, as well as abroad), this would be certainly a good time for the supposed advantage of the doctrine of Infallibility to manifest itself. It would be helpful to all of us in this country, not simply to our distinguished, sincere, and loyal Roman Catholic citizens.

CHAPTER SIX

The Foreign Aid—Birth Control Issue

IN RECENT YEARS the problem of a Roman Catholic in the Presidency or Vice-Presidency has been either fictional or abstract. *Fictional*, in the sense that part of our populace has visualized constant phone calls and telegrams from the Vatican giving directions as to the conduct of American affairs or specific directives from the "hierarchy" (with no clear picture as to who these people are or how they operate). *Abstract*, in that there has been no fresh issue which has brought this question into focus. Then, right in the midst of a certain uneasiness—generally inarticulate—about a Roman Catholic's becoming President, the Roman Catholic Bishops took the whole matter out of fiction and abstraction. They issued for release last Thanksgiving Day a statement which brought right into the realm of politics and foreign policy a matter which almost all Roman Catholics and others had heretofore thought of as only one of private morals. It was at once made evident to the whole Nation that a candidate's religion may well have something to do with the choice of the individual voter as to whom he wishes to have at the helm of the Nation.

The Bishops' Statement

First, as to the content of this statement. The Bishops said:

> For the past several years, a campaign of propaganda has been gaining momentum to influence international, national, and personal opinion in favor of birth prevention programs. The vehicle for this propaganda is the recently coined terror technique phrase, "population explosion." The phrase, indeed, alerts all to the attention that must be given to population pressures, but it also provides a smoke screen behind which a moral evil may be foisted on the

public and for obscuring the many factors that must be considered in this vital question.

More alarming is the present attempt of some representatives of Christian bodies who endeavor to elaborate the plan into a theological doctrine which envisages artificial birth prevention within the married state as the "will of God." Strangely too, simply because of these efforts and with callous disregard of the thinking of hundreds of millions of Christians and others who reject the position, some international and national figures have made the statement that artificial birth prevention within the married state is gradually becoming acceptable even in the Catholic Church. This is simply not true.

The perennial teaching of the Catholic Church has distinguished artificial birth prevention, which is a frustration of the marital act, from other forms of control of birth which are morally permissible. Method alone, however, is not the only question involved. Equally important is the sincere and objective examination of the motives and intentions of the couples involved, in view of the nature of the marriage contract itself. As long as due recognition is not given to these fundamental questions, there can be no genuine understanding of the problem.

At the present time, too, there is abundant evidence of a systematic, concerted effort to convince United States public opinion, legislators and policy makers that United States National agencies, as well as international bodies, should provide with public funds and support, assistance in promoting artificial birth prevention for economically under-developed countries.

United States Catholics believe that the promotion of artificial birth prevention is a morally, humanly, psychologically and politically disastrous approach to the population problem. Not only is such an approach ineffective in its own aims, but it spurns the basis of the real solution, sustained effort in a sense of human solidarity. Catholics are prepared to dedicate themselves to this effort, already so promisingly initiated in national and international circles. They will not, however, support any public assistance, either at home or abroad, to promote artificial birth prevention, abortion or sterilization whether through direct aid or by means of international organizations.

The fundamental reason for this position is the well considered objection to promoting a moral evil—an objection not founded solely on any typically or exclusively Catholic doctrine, but on the natural law and on basic ethical considerations. However, quite apart from the moral issue, there are other cogent reasons why Catholics would not wish to see any official support or even favor given such specious methods of "assistance."

The statement then proceeds to summarize certain social, political, and psychological arguments and to suggest alternate approaches to the solution of the problem, such as immigration, better distribution of food, and agricultural development.

The Importance of the Population Problem

The relevance of this statement to the forthcoming election was, of course, obvious. This was not simply a pastoral letter to the faithful, dealing with the ethics of birth control; rather the statement laid down the gauntlet in regard to a most important issue of foreign policy. And in so doing, the Bishops purported to speak for the entire Roman Catholic constituency, including, presumably, candidates for high office. Note the phraseology [italics ours], "*United States Catholics* believe that the promotion of artificial birth prevention is a morally, humanly, psychologically and politically disastrous approach to the population problem." And "*Catholics* . . . will not support any public assistance, either at home or abroad, to promote artificial birth prevention . . . whether through direct aid or by means of an international organization." The stand of candidates who fall within a category "United States Catholics" thus became an obvious concern. As one noted columnist pointed out, it has at least been made clear that the Roman Catholic Bishops were not trying hard to get a Roman Catholic into the presidency!

For a long time demographers and other social scientists have been warning us of the population explosion. Dr. Gardner M. Day has permitted us to use his helpful summary of the dimensions of the problem:

> In the first half of this century the population of the world increased from approximately 1-½ billion to 2-½ billion people. The United Nations estimates, which Dr. Kingsley Davis of the University of California, a distinguished population expert, considers to be extremely conservative, are that during half that time or in the next 25 years the population of the world will increase more than 1 billion or to 3,800,000,000 and that by the year 2000 it will almost double, reaching the colossal figure of 6,300,000,000. About 75 per cent of this increase in the second half of this century will be in the

undeveloped areas of the world. For example, the fastest rate of increase in population is south of the border. In tropical Latin America (Central America, the Caribbean and Mexico) the population is expected to jump from the present 65 million to 200 million by the end of this century. This is a three-fold increase in 40 years. It is estimated that China, which now has one quarter of the world's population or 650 million people, will by the end of the century have 1-½ billion people or as many people as the entire population of the world in 1950.

A comparison may help us to visualize what this means. The small island of Taiwan now has 10 million people in an area of 13,800 square miles. New Hampshire has ½ million people in 9,000 square miles. It is estimated that in less than 25 years the population of Taiwan will double so that the island will have 1,420 persons to each square mile. Those who have been in the East and seen people living in hovels and sleeping on the street can realize what this means by recalling that India now has only 332 persons per square mile and Japan, 648; and yet we know that these countries face severe overpopulation which in the past has been relieved by death because of wars, plagues, failure of food supplies, etc.

While undoubtedly there will be tremendous advances in man's ability to produce, preserve, and distribute food, agricultural experts see little hope of keeping up with, let alone keeping ahead of, this population explosion.

While the governments of India, Japan and other countries are striving hard to improve the living conditions of their people, even with millions of dollars of aid from the United States and other countries because of the rapid increase of population, their per-capita income remains practically static.

There has been widespread attention paid to the urgency of this problem. Several recent official government reports focused the need: the report of the President's Draper Committee, the report of the Senate Foreign Relations Committee prepared by the Stanford Research Institute, the State Department's Intelligence Report, prepared in July 1959 and made public in November. All of these reports pointed to the necessity of programs designed to reduce the level of fertility.

Early in November, CBS-TV first presented its documentary on the "Population Explosion," narrated by Howard K. Smith. This made a deep impression on millions of our people and, obviously, pointed to the need of direct population-control methods. The program ended quite appropriately with the presentation of two points of view as to the ethics of the use of contraceptives, the participants being Msgr. Irving De Blanc, Director of Family Life for the National Catholic Welfare Conference, and one of the authors of this book. There followed shortly thereafter the announcement of the formation, under the latter's chairmanship, of the National Clergymen's Advisory Committee for the Planned Parenthood Federation and the issuance by the Chairman of a statement as to the ethics of birth control and its bearing on the population problem.

It was thus quite natural, in the light of the firm position of the Roman Catholic Church against the use of any method of birth control (other than absolute continence or the "rhythm method") that, when the Roman Catholic Bishops met the week before Thanksgiving in Washington, they would address themselves to the question currently before the public. In this regard, as we have seen above, they did not fail expectations.

Reaction to the Statement

Asked for a comment on the Bishops' declaration, Dr. John C. Bennett, Dean of the Union Theological Seminary, said that it is tragic to see Roman Catholic leaders pressing a point of view on birth control which has no sound moral or religious basis and which has been rejected by most other Christian groups. He added that most non-Catholics were convinced that there was no valid moral distinction between "artificial" and "natural" birth-control methods. "If Catholic leaders persist in drawing such a definition," he said, "they should focus their energies on making the rhythm method more reliable rather than attempting to 'minimize the gravity of the population problem.'"

Because of the author's role as Chairman of the committee referred to above, the press asked him for a statement. In it, the following two points were made:

1. On the very day we give thanks to God for his gifts to this nation of abundance of freedom, the Roman Catholic hierarchy asserts a position which would condemn rapidly increasing millions of people in less fortunate parts of the world to starvation, bondage, misery, and despair. Would the Bishops deny family-planning assistance to these millions, the great majority of whom are not Roman Catholics and who want contraceptive help?

2. To what extent is the statement binding on Roman Catholic candidates for public office? (Consider for example, the role of the President in implementing the recommendations of the Draper report.) Are Roman Catholics in public office expected to give allegiance to this pronouncement in opposition to the freedom allowed by the law in practically every state (including the freedom of Roman Catholics not to use contraception), accepted medical practice on the part of the great majority of physicians, and the constitutional guarantee of religious freedom? The 310 Catholic Archbishops and Bishops of the Anglican Communion, of which my Church is a part, have asserted the moral duty of responsible family planning, encouraging the best medically approved methods, and other Churches have taken similar positions. Hence, I ask, are Roman Catholic public officials now called on to seek to contravene the positive religious obligations of millions of Christians and Jews and the profound convictions of countless others, and to defy the ethical relationship between doctor and patient, pastor and people?

The Kennedy Interview

Although the above statement did not direct the query to particular candidates, Mr. James Reston, Washington correspondent of the *New York Times,* lost no time in addressing it to the most prominent Roman Catholic aspirant for the Presidential nomination, Senator Kennedy. The questions and the answers:

Q.   The bishops of the United States have said that United States Catholics "will not support any public assistance, either at home or abroad, to promote artificial birth prevention, abortion, or sterilization, whether through direct aid or by means of international organizations." What is your position on this?

A.   I think it would be a mistake for the United States Government to attempt to advocate the limitation of the population of underdeveloped countries. This problem involves important social and economic questions which must be solved by the people of those countries themselves. For the United States to intervene on this basis would involve a kind of mean patriotism, which I think they would find most objectionable.

Q.   Is your position on this influenced in any way by the pronouncement of the sixteen Roman Catholic bishops in Washington last Wednesday?

A. My judgment on this has been held for many years, and it continues.

Q. You mean your present views are not the result of this statement by the bishops?

A. No. The question I think we all have to address ourselves to is whether the available resources of the world are increasing as fast as the population. That is the over-all question. My belief is that they are, though their management may not be.

Nevertheless, we have to be very careful about how we give advice on this subject. The United States Government does not advocate any policy concerning birth control here in the United States. Nor have we ever advocated such a policy in Western Europe. Accordingly, I think it would be the greatest psychological mistake for us to appear to advocate the limitation of the black or brown or yellow peoples whose population is increasing no faster than in the United States. They must reach decisions on these matters based on their own experience and judgment.

Q. What would be your position as President if the Indian Government, for example, decided on birth control as a matter of national policy? If they did so decide that it was in their interest to suggest limiting births in their national territory, would this in any way trouble you if you were President in giving aid to a country that followed such a policy?

A. As I said before, I believe this is a matter to be determined by the country itself. I would not think it was wise for the United States to refuse to grant assistance to a country which is pursuing a policy it feels to be in its own best interest. To do so would be a kind of intervention in their national life, which I would think was unwise.

Q. What if the Congress passed a law stating or recommending that countries receiving foreign aid should not allow their population to exceed their capacity to make the foreign aid funds effective?

A. I would base my determination as to whether I should approve such a law on my personal judgment as President as to what would be in the interest of the United States. If it became a law of the land, I would uphold it as the law of the land.

Q. What would you do if your Secretary of State and the head of the International Cooperation Administration recommended executive action suggesting birth control as a means of making foreign aid funds effective in another country?

A. Well, again I would make a judgment on that matter as to what I considered to be in the best interest of the United States.

It is to be noticed that in the fourth answer, Senator Kennedy did leave room for American assistance to a country whose internal policy included a program of contraceptive birth control. But the next day, having gone to Denver, Senator Kennedy closed this door, saying flatly: "I don't think it is in the national interest to spend funds in that manner. It is up to the country, itself." He also added that it "would be objectionable from the point of view of the United States. It would put us in a bad psychological position. It is a question that is too personal since it involves the life of each country." During the course of being interviewed by the press, he indicated that he saw no reason why the question should have been directed especially to Roman Catholic candidates (that answer would seem to be fairly obvious: it was the hierarchy of that particular Church which had just announced to the public that "United States Catholics would oppose . . ."). He added that the question "should be directed to all candidates and all public men." It promptly was. As a matter of fact, all of the prominent candidates made statements on the question, except Vice-President Nixon and Senator Majority Leader Lyndon B. Johnson.

Other Candidates' Positions

Another Roman Catholic possibility, Governor Edmund G. Brown of California, said:

> After study, I have arrived at the opinion that this country should not use economic aid funds so as to influence other nations or their peoples in their decisions on population control in any way, whether for or against.
>
> With but few exceptions, U.S. economic aid should be used for purposes decided on by the countries to which the aid was given, not by our government. I do not think population control is a proper exception.
>
> I would oppose banning aid to a country because the people of that country have chosen to embark on a population control program. I am further opposed to stipulating that no country shall use U.S. funds in such a program—just as I am opposed to this country offering funds on the specific condition that they be used for population control.

He added that "a Catholic public official has no more difficulty in this matter than a Catholic judge has in granting divorces, even though divorce is contrary to his religious belief."

Governor Nelson Rockefeller of New York, a Baptist and then a prominent Republican possibility, said:

> Like any programs worked out by the United States in cooperation with other countries, the programs are only developed at the request of the country involved. Therefore, naturally, as in a field relating to birth control, it would not be undertaken if it were offensive to the people of the country.
>
> On the other hand, if the people of the country requested technical assistance from the United States in an area where it had knowledge, it would seem to me that the United States would want to cooperate with them if it were in the interest of the other country.

Adlai Stevenson, a Unitarian, said:

> The United States should not impose birth control programs on foreign countries. But the United States should not hesitate to consider requests for aid to birth control programs in foreign countries where population growth is inimical to economic well-being.

Democratic hopeful, Senator Stuart Symington of Missouri, an Episcopalian, said:

> I approve the government's furnishing of planned parenthood information abroad where it believes the action is to the interest of our country.

Democratic Senator Hubert H. Humphrey of Minnesota, a Congregationalist, said:

> The United States should not adopt any policy which would deny information and assistance if such nations determine that it is essential to their national welfare. American foreign aid should not be denied on the basis of any country's policy relating to birth control. . . .

Several of the "dark horse candidates" also made public pronouncements on the subject, including Democratic Governor G. Mennen Williams of Michigan, an Episcopalian, and New York City's Mayor Robert F. Wagner, himself a Roman Catholic and prominently mentioned by the Democratic party as a possible Vice-Presidential nominee. Both agreed with Senator Kennedy's position. The Governor said that he agreed with Senator Kennedy that the use of federal funds to support birth-control measures probably would be objectionable. He added that the problem is a matter of self-determination in each country. The Mayor said that he agreed with Senator Kennedy that the United States should not use public funds to aid birth control in other countries and added that we have no right to enforce our will on any people. When he was asked whether he agreed with the Bishops' statement, the Mayor replied, "The position of the Bishops is the position of the Church. I think my position is clear on this when I agree with Senator Kennedy. Period."

There is at least one thing that all the candidates agree on: the United States should not force the use of contraceptives on any country. But this measure of agreement is not too helpful, since no one had ever proposed that we do so. Such a program would obviously be somewhat difficult of execution!

The President's Position

It was not surprising that at the President's next regular press conference the question was raised. Interestingly enough, especially if it is true, as reported, that the population-control recommendations were left in the Draper report at his insistence, the President took about the same position as Senator Kennedy but put it more vociferously.

Q. Sir, last July the committee studying foreign aid under Gen. (William H.) Draper made a recommendation to you that the United States should assist those countries with which it is cooperating in economic aid programs on request—in the formulation of their plans designed to deal with problems of rapid population growth. This was generally interpreted as a recommendation that this government should distribute birth control information on request. I wondered what your reaction to that report was, sir.

A. I cannot imagine anything more emphatically a subject that is not a proper political or governmental activity or function or responsibility.

This thing has, for very great denominations, a religious meaning, definite religious tenet in their own doctrine. I have no quarrel with them, as a matter of fact this being largely the Catholic Church, they are one of the groups that I admire and respect, but this has nothing to do with governmental contact with other governments. We do not intend to interfere with any other, the internal affairs of any other government, and if they want to do something which admittedly—to do something about what is admittedly a very difficult question, and almost an explosive question, that is their business. And, if they want to go to someone for help, they should go, they will go unquestionably to professional groups, not to governments. This government has no, and will not make, as far as I, as long as I am here, have a positive political doctrine in its program that has to do with this problem of birth control. That's not our business.

Queried by the press, the Chairman of the National Clergymen's Advisory Committee referred to above, replied:

The President has chosen to refuse, during the remainder of his Adminstration, to allow this nation of abundance to meet a primary need of countries who want aid toward population control to help avert increasing starvation and misery—and this in the face of the recommendation of the President's own committee (the Draper report), the report of the Senate Foreign Relations Committee by the Stanford Research Institute, the State Department's Intelligence report prepared in July and just made public, and the clear indication from the head of India's United Nations delegation and its commissioner-general for economic affairs that their country needs and wants such assistance.

In the light of this, we can only be grateful that this is a democratic country in which Congressional leaders and candidates for public office are free to declare themselves in favor of our assuming our Christian responsibilities to these less fortunate peoples.

According to reports of the press conference, the President, in discussing the religious aspect of this issue, mentioned only the position of the Roman Catholic hierarchy on the subject. I am sure that there are other leaders who, while respecting the right of this particular church to take this special position, will take into account the positive teaching to the contrary of other religious bodies. I trust public interest in the expressed attitudes on this issue of all candidates to succeed Mr. Eisenhower as President will continue.

Further reaction to the President's statement was prompt. Cass Canfield, president of Planned Parenthood, said that Mr. Eisenhower's stand was "alarming." "You cannot separate, in my opinion, population control from, say, malaria control. We help in malaria control; by that, one million lives are saved each year in India. Well, when you do something drastic and good like that, you cannot ignore the other end of the life cycle." He added: "The President's position flouts the authoritative findings of the experts in public health . . . experts in economic development . . . and experts in scientific research."

Dr. R. Norris Wilson, Director of Overseas Relief for the National Council of Churches, said that if the United States refused a request for birth-control assistance overseas, "I would feel that my country had been disgraced." He added: "The United States, through medical aid, has helped bring about the problem of overpopulation and has a moral obligation to help combat this problem . . . There is nothing immoral about family planning, any more than there is anything immoral about eliminating disease to lengthen the age of a person. The world is growing so fast now that technological advances to provide more food can't keep pace. We need contraception to allow the technological advances to catch up."

The Rev. Dr. William A. Morrison, General Secretary of the Board of Christian Education of the United Presbyterian Church in the U.S.A. said, in part, ". . . I personally believe that the United Presbyterian Church would support any governmental action which would provide birth-control information to another nation in response to its request for such assistance."

The President's position did have a defender in the Rev. Dr. Edwin T. Dahlberg, President of the National Council of Churches. He opined that nations desiring birth-prevention information should get it through private agencies and foundations rather than from the Federal government. Dr. Dahlberg's view, in turn, was challenged by the Rev. Dr. Ray Gibbons, Director of the Council for Christian Social Action of the United Church of Christ, and the Rev. Henry C. Koch, Vice-Chairman of that council, who said that it would be "to our national interest to have nations like India, which are seeking freedom and social development, able to find the assistance they seek in controlling their population increase."

Dr. Gibbons and Mr. Koch also disputed Dr. Dahlberg's thesis that a Roman Catholic President could let his conscience be his guide in passing on a birth-control bill: "It is well that we respect the rights of individual consciences in the United States, but when the President of the United States signs bills and establishes the policy of this government towards other governments, he must necessarily act in the national interest. If his private conscience does not permit him to do what the national interest requires, he cannot fulfill his office."

Rabbi Maurice N. Eisendrath, President of the United Hebrew Congregations [Reformed] pointed out that "in an apparent effort to avoid offense to any religious group, President Eisenhower has evaded one of the gravest problems of our time." He added:

I do not believe that one can examine the problem of mushrooming populations without frank consideration of the question of birth control. While I respect the position of the Roman Catholic Church and will vigorously defend their right to express the teachings of the church, I feel that no Church has the right to impose its own dogma on the American people or the foreign policy of this nation.

To conduct a foreign policy in the light of this population explosion without making available necessary medical knowledge to the peoples of the world who desire it is to nullify all that we seek to do in our generous programs of foreign aid and technical assistance.

The Protestant Council of the City of New York, which earlier in 1959 had led a successful fight to make birth-control information available in the hospitals of New York City, issued the following statement: "It is regrettable that the President has ignored the beliefs and teachings of millions of Americans who belong to our Protestant Communions. Protestants believe that birth control, or planned parenthood, practiced in Christian conscience, fulfills, rather than violates, the Will of God." It said that the morally proper use of medically approved contraceptives contributes to the social, economic, and spiritual welfare of the home and to the physical and mental welfare of parents and children. "Because Protestants do have these beliefs," the statement continued, "it is proper that their views be considered in any action proposed by our government related to birth control, and it is also proper for Americans to ask candidates who seek public office what they will do in various situations that relate to their religious convictions." The New York Board of Rabbis, representing 700 Orthodox, Conservative, and Reformed congregations in the Metropolitan area, expressed the feeling that birth-control aid should be made available to countries which "in pursuit of their own considered welfare" request such aid.

Dean John C. Bennett, who has previously been quoted in response to the statement of the Roman Catholic Bishops, also responded to the President's statement:

Many Protestants regard the use of contraceptives for responsible birth control as a matter of conscience, and not as a concession to sin. This view is widely held by others as well and I feel it was disregarded by President Eisenhower in making his statement on the matter . . . It is unfortunate that President Eisenhower apparently has foreclosed our cooperation and done so by defining the issue as religious. The implications are disturbing: If strong religious opinion can make any act impossible as a policy of government, we will obviously be hampered and eventually move nowhere.

In the midst of this controversy, the National Council of the Protestant Episcopal Church was holding its quarterly meeting. Taking account of the political issue which had been raised, and recognizing "the profound differences among Christians concerning the nature and purposes of human sexuality and the family," the Council set forth anew the Church's position on the matter and urged "members of the Church as citizens to press through their governments and through social, educational, and international agencies, for measures aimed at relieving problems of population growth, particularly in areas of acute overpopulation."

Earlier, the Presiding Bishop, the Rt. Rev. Arthur Lichtenberger, while affirming that a candidate's religion should not be made a test of his qualifications for the Presidency, recognized the foreign-aid issue as a "legitimate national concern," and compared the question of supplying birth-control information upon request to overpopulated areas to that of giving assistance in preventing floods in India. "I don't see how we can refuse to respond to requests of this type either," he said. "If the government of our country is legitimately concerned with the health and welfare of people in other countries, then birth-control information is its legitimate concern also."

Scores of other Church leaders, including the President of the United Presbyterian Women, responded in a similar vein.

The Columnists Are Heard From

In the meanwhile, a large literature on the subject had been developed by the newspaper columnists and editorial writers and other spokesmen. As would be expected, both points of view found both support and criticism. In the statements in general support of both the President and Senator Kennedy six points have come to the fore:

1. *It is unfortunate that the religious issue has been dragged into the*

campaign. As most writers made clear, legitimate differences in the ethics of birth control were brought into the political sphere, not by Protestants or Jews but by the Roman Catholic Bishops. Some went on to suggest that the mere fact a public issue had religious implications meant that it was an inappropriate issue for consideration in the selection of candidates. Here, for example, David Lawrence invoked the "religious test" prohibition in the Constitution. We believe that we have already sufficiently covered this point in Chapter One: in short, a blanket opposition in the mind of a voter, or of a party or organization to the election of a man, simply because he is of a given religious faith, is both wrong and contrary to the spirit of the "religious test" provision; but the views of candidates upon important issues are relevant even if the differences of views are grounded in differences of religious conviction. Where the ecclesiastical leadership of a given Church deliberately brought before the public what it would expect its members to hold in regard to a particular public issue, it is entirely to the point to know how candidates of that faith would act when faced with decision-making in a given area.

2. *This nation should not force birth control on other nations.* This is a red herring: in all the reams of reported discussions on the subject, no one has to date ever so much as suggested such a program. Some of the candidates have also made this point. But this is not the question. All through the debate the question has been and is: In connection with our foreign-aid program, will we or will we not ban technical assistance to birth control by medically accepted methods to those nations who desire such assistance where such programs are a part of their internal policy?

3. *There are other methods of meeting the population explosion problem.* In their statement, the Roman Catholic Bishops were not oblivious to the needs of the undeveloped nations whose populations exceed existing resources. In fact, they well summarized other remedies which should certainly commend themselves for study and action. Here is not a matter of either/or but of both/and. When we perceive any grave problem affecting the destinies of millions of people, are we justified in rejecting any legitimate approach to its rapid solutions simply on the grounds that a particular religious minority does not regard the method as legitimate, especially where the religious convictions of those so to be served are not opposed to the particular method? It may well be true, as some have suggested, that in decades

ahead food and other basic necessities will be increased to meet the needs of expanding populations in these areas (but even then there will be need of family planning on the part of particular couples, just as there is in this country with ample material means). But *now* ample resources are desperately lacking, and the population is increasing in geometric proportions. In the ethical systems held by most Americans, we are called upon to make decisions in terms of the situation at hand, not in terms of some "ideal" order of things. Obviously, no one could recommend a method of solution which is evil per se; but the fact is that the majority of American citizens simply do not believe that contraception is evil—indeed, they believe that it is good in appropriate circumstances.

4. *The issue is "academic."* A few columnists and some editorials made this point. Mr. Truman said, "It's a false issue so far as the Presidency is concerned. They always get a false issue to break up the Democratic party before a convention." But, interestingly enough, he and his fellow members of the Democratic Advisory Council urged creation of a "National Peace Agency" which would study, among other things, "overpopulation, including acceptable methods of dealing with over-rapid population expansion."

It is true that the United States today does not supply foreign aid toward contraception. But this does not mean that it should not, when requested by nations in need of such aid. Now there was a time when this nation supplied no foreign aid at all. Suppose at such a time it were recommended by three important government committees (as in the case of the reports favoring aid on population control) that we establish a foreign-aid program, and an isolationist group issued an attack on the idea (as the Roman Catholic Bishops did on the population control question). When these attacks were answered by other citizens, would it have been to the point for columnists and politicians to say, "the question is academic, because the United States has never provided any foreign aid anyway?"

It is true that any desire or possibility of providing such aid would depend upon a desire for it by a given nation. In the case of aid toward contraception it would be a nation with a problem of overpopulation and an internal policy to that end. But during the very course of this discussion, Indian leaders have made clear that they would appreciate such aid, which they desperately need, being unable to handle the problem themselves. More than that, India, Japan, and other nations already have a settled internal policy in favor of contraception.

5. *This type of aid should come from private agencies.* Some others have taken the line that if these other nations wish this help, they should seek it through outside private agencies rather than from the United States government. First, to recognize the good half-truth of these statements: private agencies have all along been doing wonderful work in assisting underdeveloped countries in the placement of refugees, in the meeting of disaster, etc. Whatever the government has done or will do in our own foreign aid, of course, it would not—and should not—eliminate the important role of nongovernmental agencies, church and secular. As to the particular problem under discussion, Protestant medical missionaries have in many places been assisting families with contraceptive advice. Even before World War II, medical missionaries in China gave couples advice on how to limit the size of their families. Dr. Fred G. Scovel, Secretary of the Christian Medical Council of the National Council of Churches and himself a medical missionary for thirty years, has said that wherever Protestant doctors and nurses are at work in the foreign field, their help in family planning is requested. Only recently a Lutheran Church in India asked the United Lutheran Church in America to send additional medical missionaries to India to teach planned parenthood and to establish birth-control clinics in hospitals and medical centers. Such aid, where requested, is given in Roman Catholic countries. The Rev. Dr. Truman B. Douglass, Executive Vice-President of the Board of Home Missions of the Congregational Christian Churches, reported that hundreds of Roman Catholic women are participating in an experiment with oral contraceptives at the Board's Ryder Hospital in Puerto Rico. He said that the hospital's service to the cause of population control is far from being antireligious; it is a positive expression of Christian compassion and humanitarian concern. The experiment began two years ago with 450 patients, "a vast majority of whom are Roman Catholics. All women who have taken the pills according to the directions of physicians at the hospital have had success in not conceiving."

But why, in this realm alone, should we leave the matter entirely to private agencies? Private agencies, church and other groups have played a most important role in the resettlement of refugees, but obviously the program has been much more successful because the respective governments of the United Nations have been heavily involved in it—both financially and by way of personnel. The same is true of "death control," through the various governmental and nongovernmental programs toward the elimination of disease. The same has been true of famine control and aid in the case of disasters. It would be at least a logical (although we do not think sound) argument to say that all foreign aid should be left to private agencies; but it is not logical to urge that in this particular aspect of the solution of the problems of underdeveloped and overpopulated countries, the government should have no part, the U.N. should have no part, but that the private agencies should have to meet the need unaided.

Among those who have made the "private agency point" are some who really favor contraceptive population control; the reason for their preference for private agencies as a means of providing it is their recognition of the fact that one religious group in the country is opposed to the whole idea. But we are sure that none of these would want to apply this disinvolvement of the government in other fields of activity where it happens that a religious group is opposed to the policy involved. A number of denominations oppose war or armaments of any kind, and their adherents are just as convinced as to the immorality of the implements of war as Roman Catholics are of the implements of birth control. Yet no one has suggested that arms be supplied to friendly nations needing them—but only by private agencies. Christian Scientists are convinced that disease does not exist; yet, in spite of our respect for their convictions, we do not leave medical assistance to other nations simply to private agencies; in fact, Christian Scientists are required to pay their share of tax money to support our extensive medical-aid programs. Orthodox Jews believe that the use of pork is contrary to God's eternal Law; yet our government does not hesitate to supply pork abroad—and Orthodox Jews, through their taxes, help pay for the porcine export. The limit of the legal protection of the rights of these minority groups is that, recognizing "conscientious objection," we do not force members of the pacifist churches to take up arms nor require Christian Scientists to take medicine for malaria nor force Jews to eat pork. Thus it should be sufficient protection of his rights that no Roman Catholic is forced—or even urged—by the government to use contraceptive devices.

6. *It is not an important question.* This is a final point that has been made in the attempt to sweep the issue under the rug. We would be

the first to agree (as we have spelled out in Chapter One) that a Presidential candidate's view on this question should not be the sole determinative factor in the decision to vote for or against him. On the other hand, we would underline the fact that, quite apart from the merits of the two sides of the case, the question is one of the two or three most important issues confronting our nation at the present time. There are many of us who feel that the safety of the world's future depends on a solution now to two "explosion" problems—nuclear and population. Even if we find some way to eliminate the threat of the former, the safety of the world could be gravely imperiled by the latter. In fact, failure to solve the latter problem may make it impossible to solve the former: the whole history of mankind has shown that when a given geographical area cannot supply sufficient available food and other resources for its population, the population presses against its borders; it has also shown that when people are sufficiently desperate they will embrace any -ism, even one as false as Communism.

As to why we should be concerned as to how candidates feel on such a question, let us look at an analogous issue. I think that we would all agree that one of the important issues before the nation is the farm program. Last fall, *Life* magazine devoted a number of pages to setting forth the views of the various candidates on this question. No one thought it unworthy for farmers and for the citizenry generally to be concerned as to these views. In regard to such considerations no one has thrown up the words "special interests," "bigotry," "unimportant." And no one interested in the farm question has been satisfied with such simple statements by a candidate as: "I will do what I think best in the public interest," or "I will obey my oath of office," or "I will put nothing higher than my allegiance to my country." Such general patriotic sentiments (which undoubtedly all of the Presidential candidates mean most sincerely) would not be enough to satisfy the voters: they want to know in clear terms where each of the candidates stands on the farm program, so that they may bear this in mind when they cast their ballots.

Many Americans obviously, feel the same way about the foreign aid-birth control issue.

CHAPTER SEVEN

Dead Issues—More or Less

THE TITLE WOULD SEEM to afford the readers sufficient excuse to skip the chapter, but we urge them to tarry. Some understanding of the issues to be summarized is important to the understanding of the whole complex of the situation. Further, as anyone who follows the papers and newsmagazines knows, the political configuration can change very quickly, and some incident—perhaps an apparently totally unconnected event—may stir up the embers of issues that many, including the authors, have assumed are dying or dead. We would not trouble you if the questions here discussed were merely passing incidents in some past time. But actually they have remained rather perennial questions, more vivid at some times than at others. The title of the chapter simply reflects two things: (1) in comparison to the general Church-State issue, and the issue in the foreign-policy question of technical assistance in regard to birth control in over-populated countries, the issues next to be discussed fall into the shadows; and (2) if Election Day were as of the time of this writing, the authors themselves would give very little weight to these other issues. But this does not mean that certain readers would not; nor does it mean that by the time the book is within hard covers, or before the summer conventions, or before the fall elections, one or another of these questions may not have assumed major proportions. At the moment we are discussing them simply for the record.

There are other issues, actual or potential; but the ones here to be discussed are: (1) The problem of allegiance to a foreign state; (2) the question of diplomatic representation to the Vatican; and (3) the matter of federal aid to parochial schools.

Allegiance to a Foreign Power

This one is a real red herring. But concern about it on the part of some Americans is understandable, since the history of the temporal authority of the Papacy is confusing, even to the experts; and contributing to the confusion of the citizen used to American institutions is the fact that the Popes themselves so long insisted that temporal authority is essential to their divine office. How much the maintenance of this position is on the "infallible" side or the "human" side of the Papacy we leave for Roman Catholic theologians and apologists to decide. The plain fact is that today the Pope is both the head of a Church (comparable to the Patriarch of Constantinople and the Archbishop of Canterbury) and the head of a State (comparable to the Prince of Monaco and the Prince of Andorra). It is a small one, to be sure, but one with independent sovereignty. It has no army (save the picturesque Swiss Guard), navy, or air force; it has no industry nor any commerce, beyond that comparable to an army "post exchange." It does have coinage and postage (benefitting mostly numismatists and philatelists), diplomatic relations, and full theoretical—and much practical—freedom from external control. Among the Cardinals, who represent the administrative officialdom, there is some mixture of functions between large Church and small State.

Now everyone would agree, including Roman Catholics, that since no American citizen is supposed to have an allegiance to another nation, a fortiori the President or the Vice-President should not have. Of course, a devout and loyal Roman Catholic does have an allegiance to the Pope. And because of the hierarchical and authoritarian nature of the Roman Catholic Church, his allegiance is doubtless somewhat more vivid and direct than the allegiance to the ecclesiastical officials of other churches, in which the authority is generally more diffused. The Bishop of the Episcopal Diocese of California, for example, expects a measure of allegiance from the priests and laity of his Diocese; the Presiding Bishop of our Church, I am sure, counts on a measure of allegiance from all the Episcopalians, clergy and lay, in the country; and certainly part of the moral support of the Archbishop of Canterbury in his concern for the whole Anglican communion is a sense of having a measure of allegiance from the thirty million Anglicans throughout the world. But none of the prelates mentioned have—or claim—infallibility as to even their most official decrees, nor, as to other issuances, do they have the expectation of universal "interior assent" —nor, for that matter, freedom from external criticism, within or without the Church. Some would call this weakness, some would call it strength; but in any case, it is *different* than the situation of the Bishop of Rome in the Roman Catholic ethos.

Nevertheless, assuming the maximum of devotion to the Pope on the part of a Roman Catholic political official, in his mind his allegiance is not of a different character (though perhaps greater in intensity) than the loyalty referred to above in the case of Episcopalians. In other words, allegiance to Papal authority is part of his religion, not part of his political thinking or commitments. He doubtless knows that the Pope is also sovereign of an area much smaller than Brooklyn; but it is not to that miniscule nation nor to its sovereign that he directs his allegiance.

Vatican City Has no International Aims

The fact is that Vatican City, as a geographical entity, has no international aims or possibilities (apart from the maintenance of its existence) which could create a compromising situation for a citizen of another State. Speaking in historical perspective, this tiny principality can be viewed either as a belated "consolation prize" to the Pope as the final outcome of the contest involved in the unification of Italy or (by analogy to the role of the District of Columbia) as a practical way of insuring the independence, in relation to the whole of the Roman Catholic Church, of the head of that Church, who obviously must have his See in some given part of the world. That this is not strictly necessary to the Papacy (though not all Popes have realized this) is clear from the ability of the earlier Bishops of Rome, before the time of Gregory the Great, to function without any civil authority whatsoever and, by the ability of the fifteenth-century Popes, to rule ecclesiastically out of Avignon.

But there is no necessity for "outsiders" to weigh all this. The facts are that there is such a small piece of land under autonomous authority and that it is difficult to conceive of any issue in which Vatican City would be involved in a major contest between nations which would make remotely relevant an American role in the matter. But even should such an unimaginable issue occur, it is quite clear that in the mind of the average Roman Catholic (and this would presumably include those holding high office) their allegiance to Vatican City in such matters could not be counted on (except on the merits of the issue itself).

What those who raise this question (except where it is a shibboleth of prejudice) have in mind would have been much more relevant during the period when the Pope was sovereign of a good portion of central Italy, then called "the Papal States." But the record shows that during this period American Roman Catholics were by no means united in support of the Pope's temporal claims; in fact, even Roman Catholic Bishops were somewhat diffident about support of the Pope at this juncture. The nation involved was one of the worst administered in Europe, though Pius IX was just beginning to introduce some reforms. Thanks to the offices—good or bad—of Garibaldi, he was relieved of the necessity of carrying them through; and actually no one has a right to expect too much of a priest trying to run a small country on the side! Bishops and denominational officials of other churches have not always found themselves successful in running the temporal affairs of even their ecclesiastical jurisdictions. Knowing something of the episcopate, we expect that the Bishops of Rome in recent times have been privately grateful (whether or not it is possible to say this publicly) that their civil authority has been cut down to a minimum. Whether Italy has been entirely well run since is not the point: at least how it is run is not on their consciences! Whereas, the way the Papal States were run was. Out of personal feeling we can aver: running a Church—or Diocese of the same—is difficult enough.

In other words, this *isn't* a question. In case any of you are unconvinced, let's take an analogy. Many Jews (especially Zionists—but in a somewhat more critical way other Jews—and many Christians, including the non-Zionist episcopal author of this book) have a great devotion to the state of Israel. We hope it will prosper, and many of us have contributed in our own way toward its fulfillment. But let's focus the question on the "religious Zionist," for whom the ultimate fulfillment of Israel is grounded in his religion. Should he on a given issue put the interest of Israel ahead of the interest of the United States in his decision-making as far as his vote and political activity are concerned, then everyone (perhaps even he) would agree that this is disloyalty to his nation. But to the degree that his religiously-motivated enthusiasm for Israel causes him to further a cause which is relatively independent of our national interest, or which, either through reason or rationalization, he sees as consistent with our national interest, we cannot declare him disloyal to the United States just because of his Israeli interests.

Whether from religious ties or plain nostalgia, the fact is that even ethnic origins quite naturally (and without any legitimate condemnation) result in a certain interest in other nations. It would be strange indeed—almost heartless—if a second-generation Swede had no interest in the prosperity of Sweden among the nations of the earth. The interest in Great Britain of those in this country of English origin is not only not condemned but an honorable place is given to societies meant to further this interest (e.g., the English-Speaking Union and the Pilgrims), and they have in their way helped maintain a continuing liaison (despite many crises) between the two principal nations which have a large measure of Anglo-Saxon culture, speech, and institutions.

All such ties and motivations are good, provided the basic loyalty to the United States—as far as the international political scene goes—can be trusted. Therefore, concern on this much-agitated point should be dismissed.

What About the Vatican's Political Interests?

Many who will agree on this might still raise a problem that sounds somewhat the same but is really quite different. Granted that Vatican *City* has no particular political interests to be furthered, the Vatican has a complicated set of political interests throughout the world: the maintenance of its preferred (and sometimes almost exclusive) status in "Catholic States"; the retention and (so far as may be) the strengthening of its Concordats with such states and with others; its eagerness that the *status quo* be maintained in nations where the Roman Catholic Church is treated as it would wish; on occasion, its desire, where it is not so treated, that the existing regime be overthrown; and, of course, the Church's antagonism to world-wide Communism.

Sometimes the political position of the Vatican concurs with what is deemed the best American foreign policy; but it need not necessarily. Hence, the question is: would a Roman Catholic President be likely to take his cue on such an issue from the Vatican or would he be guided by a sincere endeavor to discern our national interest and the good of the nations concerned?

This is not easy to answer. It was not a Roman Catholic but an Episcopalian President, Franklin D. Roosevelt, who laid on the legitimate government of Spain an arms embargo which was the principal factor enabling the Vatican-supported revolutionaries to overthrow the regime. True, at that time, there was considerable American Roman Catholic pressure—journalistic and otherwise—in favor of the embargo; but it would be entirely speculative to assess whether this pressure would have been greater or less on a Roman Catholic President. It is not entirely certain, had the President at that time been a Roman Catholic, that he would have taken the same position, since there was a body of Roman Catholic opinion (articulate, for example, in the pages of *Commonweal*) which was far from enthusiastic about the Franco cause.

Obviously, whatever any President would do in any such realm would be verbalized in terms of "the best interests of our nation." Precisely what motivation—or mixture of motives—might lie behind the Presidential action, we could never get at without the aid of a psychoanalyst. The best we can hope for here is to know the particular stand of a given candidate upon a specific set of issues. And, as to possible future issues, we must rely upon trust of the man himself. As to the suggestion that a Roman Catholic President might just naturally tend to be more sympathetic to the "Vatican line," we can grant this possibility but at the same time point out that there is another possibility: he might, on the contrary, feel constrained to "lean over backward" to avoid any appearance of such an inclination.

Diplomatic Representation to the Vatican

It is in the context of the discussion of the previous point that this issue should be understood. In other words, in reaching any judgment on the question, we must keep in mind the distinction between a vast Church and a tiny State.

But before anyone burdens himself with the issue as such, it is important to note that we do not at present have any such representation at the Holy See; nor does President Eisenhower apparently have in mind such a step; nor has any candidate indicated such a desire. In fact, the principal Roman Catholic candidate, Senator Kennedy, has declared his opposition to the idea.

It is true that from 1848 to 1867 we had a chargé-d'affaires and later a Minister Resident to the Papal States. An incidental fact, as the record shows, is that part of the purpose was to please American Roman Catholic citizens; but the primary fact is that at that time the temporal holdings of the Vatican constituted a sizeable country. Although it would not appear that during any of this time we had much trade or significant political problems with the Papal States, it is clear that, as to the relationship, only blind prejudice could call it a violation of our tradition of the separation of Church and State. The point is emphasized by the nature of the careful instructions from the Secretaries of State to the envoys as to their exact role. For example, James Buchanan in 1848 issued the following instructions to the first chargé:

> Your efforts therefore will be devoted exclusively to the cultivation of the most friendly civil relations with the Papal Government, and to the extension of commerce between the two countries. You will carefully avoid even the appearance of interfering in ecclesiastical questions, whether these relate to the United States or any other portion of the world. It may be proper, should you deem it advisable, to make these views known, on some suitable occasion, to the Papal Government; so that there may be no mistake or misunderstanding on this subject.[1]

The exact nature of the relationship, resting purely on the political nature of the Papal States, was also emphasized in instructions from Secretary William H. Seward in 1862 to the Hon. Richard M. Blatchford when he was appointed Minister.

> . . . This government, in 1848, wisely determined that while it maintained representatives in the capitals of every other civilized State, and even in the capitals of many semi-civilized States, who reject the whole Christian religion, it is neither wise nor necessary to exclude Rome from the circle of our diplomatic intercourse . . . So far as spiritual or ecclesiastical matters enter into the question they are beyond your province, for you are political representative only.[2]

Because of misunderstandings as to the difficulty, within the provisions of the law of the Papal States which did not allow worship by Protestant "sects," of providing Protestant services for Americans residing in or visiting the Holy City, and because of growing sympathy with the aspirations of Italians for a united Italy, in 1867 Congress refused to appropriate any further money for the mission, and it ceased to exist.

At no time during this period, did the Papal State send a Nuncio to the United States. When Leo XIII developed the idea of sending an unofficial (as far as the State is concerned) representative to

Washington, the American hierarchy was almost unanimously opposed. When the representative arrived, bearing to the Chicago World's Fair documents dealing with the Columbian voyages, and indicated to American Bishops that the Pope wished him to remain in America as his representative, Cardinal Gibbons wrote the Pope thanking him for sending his representative on this "temporary mission."[3] Nevertheless, the next month the apostolic delegation was established by Papal action.

The Roosevelt Experiment

But by 1939 much water had gone over the dam. In 1938 an impressive new building for the Apostolic Delegation was opened on Embassy Row in Washington, the Ambassador to the Court of St. James had been sent by President Roosevelt as his personal representative to the coronation of Pius XII, and in December of the same year (1939) Mr. Roosevelt sent his "personal representative" to the Vatican. But just as the American hierarchy had sought to discourage the sending of an apostolic delegate here, the Vatican discouraged a regular diplomatic relationship to the United States: in March of the same year, a spokesman of the Vatican rejoiced in the position of Roman Catholics in the United States and indicated that the exchange of diplomatic representation "would raise a multitude of difficult and embarrassing questions [prophecy indeed!]."[4]

The appointment of a distinguished American Episcopalian to this post for the duration of the war and as a representative of the President for cooperation in European peace moves won wide support—and wide criticism. However, for the future posture of the issue it is unfortunate that the President did not sufficiently distinguish the Vatican City as a state and the Roman Catholic Curia as an international ecclesiastical H.Q. But one cannot criticize F.D.R. too blithely. There is a dilemma in the whole situation.

However truncated the political character and functions of Vatican City as a state may be, it is still an independent sovereignty, and no American, however anti-Roman Catholic he may be, could have any legitimate ground of objection to our sending some form of diplomatic representation to this tiny state. The fact that its Prince is also the head of a world religion should not militate against the governmental basis for the action (whatever the motives behind the step: as has been indicated above, the step taken in 1848 had as part of its basis the pleasing of American Roman Catholics). The fact that there might be little for such a diplomatic representative to do, particularly if he remained within the purely political confines defined by the Secretaries of State when we had such regular diplomatic representation, is not entirely to the point; our diplomatic representatives in a number of small countries have little to do.

But any possible value, in terms of the large interests of the United States, in sending a person of top diplomatic rank (and of top caliber —and this certainly accurately describes Mr. Taylor) to so tiny a state really rests on the fact that the Pope is the head of a large world religious organization. This is obviously what Mr. Roosevelt had in mind. Simultaneously with his official letter to Mr. Myron Taylor asking him to represent him (and, indirectly, us) at the Vatican, the President sent an almost identical letter to the President of the Federal Council of Churches (Dr. George A. Buttrick) and the President of the Jewish Theological Seminary (Rabbi Cyrus Adler). To them he suggested *en passant* that "it would give me great satisfaction if you would, from time to time, come to Washington to discuss the problems which all of us have on our minds, in order that our parallel endeavors for peace and the alleviation of suffering may be assisted."[5] (There is no evidence that this invitation produced much fruit nor was it likely to: such a comment had about the same effect as a casual comment to an acquaintance: "We must get together sometime.") Nevertheless, the "running in" of these two symbolic, representative figures, while it was meant to smooth the way for the simultaneous provision for Vatican representation, "let the cat out of the bag." It was because Eugenio Pacelli was His Holiness the Pope, not because he was the Prince of a tiny state, that a figure of the rank of Ambassador Extraordinary was sent to the Vatican.

The sharp distinction made above has less consequence as to nations without a firm doctrine of the separation of Church and State. Thus argument from precedent as to various "Catholic states" and other nations (such as England and Germany) is of no particular relevance. No American, aware of our constitutional traditions, could be in favor of an Ambassador to the Pope as a religious leader. On the other hand, no American (whatever his prejudices) could make a decent argument against our sending to Vatican City a consul or chargé of about the same rank or professional stature as we might send to Andorra or Monaco. Any question raised about this should have no religious implications: it would simply be a question as to whether it was a wise expenditure of governmental money, considering the fact that our trade relations and our meeting the needs of applicants for visas, etc., in Vatican City might well be limited indeed. Here it might be suggested by a neutral "efficiency expert" that the American consular set-up in Rome might, with due recognition of the separate sovereignty of the Vatican City, do double duty (just as certain consular and diplomatic officials serve both Israel and Jordan, the Mandelbaum Gate being open to them by mutual agreement; there is even less difficulty in entering Vatican City from Rome, as any tourist knows).

But it has been persistently suggested that there is a larger value to our country in such representation, in terms of "Intelligence," mutual consultation as to policies, influence—in our interest—on the Church's political stance, etc. It can be granted that, in regard to any such possible values, the Roman Catholic Church is more significant than other churches. But, insofar as the idea has value, no one can say that similar relationships with other churches would have no point; this, under the spirit and letter of the prohibition of the First Amendment against "establishment" of religion (regardless of the Roman Catholic Church's self-estimate in relation to other bodies), is a matter of *difference in degree*, not a *difference in kind*.

An Alternative Proposal—or Reductio ad Absurdum

To avoid confusion, it might be well to devise a new (and, of course, dignified and suitably honorific) title for such liaison officers. As Anglicans, we would be the last to oppose the sending of such an envoy to Lambeth—especially in light of the fact that an American citizen, the Rt. Rev. Stephen F. Bayne, Jr., until recently our Bishop in Western Washington, recently assumed his duties as Executive Officer of the Anglican Communion, serving directly under the Archbishop of Canterbury. This nation might thereby indeed gain much by way of information and support at the seat of the *primus inter pares* of 35,000,000 Christians. Sending such an envoy to Geneva as an "ear" and "mouth" in relationship to the vast work of the World Council of Churches, which represents a huge body of people throughout the world, might serve our nation well. The presence of such an official personality in Istanbul, seeking to develop relationships of hearing and talking with the ecumenical Patriarch of all Eastern

Orthodox Christians, might be far from useless (though the recent unwillingness of President Eisenhower, in Istanbul anyway, to spend even ten minutes with the ecumenical Patriarch after having spent an hour with the Pope did not reflect that the present leadership of this country would regard this as useful). Just to whom to send a leader of world Jewry would take further study, although for symbolic purposes it might be appropriate to send such a liaison officer to Jerusalem where he might establish a pattern of conversations with the Chief Rabbi.

But this would leave still to be settled similar representation to churches which are not parts of world communions and which are strictly American. I am sure that space could be found for an envoy in the large, new, modern building erected by the National Council of Churches on Riverside Drive, New York City, and the presence of such a person, well qualified, might not only serve our government's interests, but it might save the N.C.C. some of its lobbying (and I use this word in a positive—and good—sense) in Washington. But unfortunately for some Protestant Churches who regard the N.C.C. as the hotbed of heresy and Communism, it would be necessary to send some member of the diplomatic corps to the American Council of Churches. But a third man would still be needed; there is an in-between group, the National Association of Evangelicals. But even then provision would have to be made for the Christian Scientists, by the sending of an official delegate to the Mother Church in Boston, and an envoy would have to be sent to Utah, so that Mormonism might not be neglected. And so on.

The above is said partially with tongue in cheek but only partially so. Our government has a lot more to learn from the various religious bodies represented in our country than it, or the churches, have yet realized. But the point we are trying to make, for the purposes of the present issue, should be obvious enough. Now that the Pope does not have temporal jurisdiction over a third of Italy, the problem of official representation to Vatican City should be a matter of about the same stature as the commissioning of consular representation to San Marino. Hence, if there is a reason, in the minds of the State Department and the President, for naming a separate official—of suitable unimportance—to Vatican City, there can be no legitimate objection as far as principle is concerned. But when it comes to representation to the Pope on the basis of his headship of a Church, whatever value there may be in such, then there should be representation all round. Such a plan would be complicated, as we have suggested; nevertheless, this is the only basis consistent with American principles on which such representation could be established.

In this regard, Senator Kennedy is no problem; he has clearly declared himself against such representation to the Vatican. But in solicitation of the views of any other Roman Catholic candidate for the Presidency (or for the Vice-Presidency; as we have indicated in Chapter One, this is also of importance), it is time that the question be raised in more specific terms than it has been heretofore, and here we suggest the questions (in case anyone implies we have no right to ask questions, we are citizens too, quite apart from the episcopal and capitular titles we bear, in what, so far as the United States Constitution is concerned, is purely an "informal" and incorporated organization):

1. "Do you favor diplomatic and/or consular representation to Vatican City on a basis appropriate to its size and military and commercial significance?" If the candidate says "Yes," please don't hold it against him, even if you think the United States will not receive benefits proportionate to the money spent. Taxes are so high now that a little wasted money here and there should not figure too much in the campaign!

2. "Do you favor sending an Ambassador to the Pope, the head of an important world religion?" If he says "Yes," don't rule him out immediately, but simply ask him another question: "Then, what is your plan to arrange for diplomatic representation to all the other faiths represented by American citizens?"

We believe if the questions are put this way the issue will wash out —both with the candidate and the public.

Federal Aid to Parochial Schools

Most citizens concerned with the future of education in this country (especially in the face of the official and unofficial reports as to the increasing success of the Soviet educational system and particularly as to their professional competence in the more threatening fields, e.g., nuclear physics) are apostles for some form of federal aid to education. But, there are two political obstacles to the achievement of this end: (1) the unwillingness (we think justified) of the majority of Congress to grant this aid to school districts not complying with the Constitution as interpreted by our highest court, i.e., those who insist on continuing segregation; (2) the opposition to such a measure on the part of Roman Catholics (and some others) in each House to the measure unless equal grants are provided for parochial schools. The Congressional deadlock over this question has been manifest over recent years, and we doubt very much if the President could do very much about it, regardless of his religious faith or of his views on each specific question involved.

Here we have a basic question of policy which divides Americans. As officials of a Church which does not regard it as "un-American" to run Church schools, we would defend the existence of a pluralistic school system as a legitimate part of a pluralistic society. Further, we would say that a grant of governmental financial aid to all schools which meet certain minimum standards (which would not need to be very high to meet the standard of the public schools in some areas), while possibly unfeasible from both practical and political points of view, would nevertheless not be intrinsically "un-American"; such plans obtain—however they are to be evaluated—in such democratic countries as Scotland and Holland.

Yet, leaving now the realm of theory, we all know that any such plan would operate principally to the financial advantage of a single minority group, since no religious body in this country has a day-school system comparable to the size of the Roman Catholic school system. The growth of parish day schools sponsored by non-Roman Catholic churches has been phenomenal in the last decade; nevertheless, should a federal aid program including parochial schools be adopted right now, one religious group would come out way ahead of all the rest. This numerical advantage (and this is a sociological, rather than an ideological, matter) is a legitimate concern. Hence different candidates and voters might well fall into three classes:

(1) Those who feel that the public school is the only type of education to be encouraged in American life. (If one takes this position he can not rely too heavily on historical American principles, since public schools came on the scene rather late, and were not intended to occupy the entire educational field.)[6] (2) Those who believe, on ideological or practical grounds, that this country would be better off with a pluralistic school system, like that of Scotland with its Church of Scotland, Episcopal Church of Scotland, Roman Catholic, and secular schools, all supported by the government—the whole business sup-

ported out of tax money (again a perfectly legitimate democratic position, assuming no preference for any religious body).[7] (3) Those who in theory would recognize the legitimacy of position (2), but who recognize pragmatically that the adoption now of such a scheme would in fact favor one church.

Again, as in the case of the last issue, we are not suggesting or arguing which position a voter should take; but rather are seeking to set forth the framework in which the question should be asked any given candidate. The way a voter, whatever his view, assesses the answer a candidate gives on such questions is certainly a legitimate factor for him in his total estimate of the candidate, when it comes to expressing his decision through the ballot box. But the voter has no moral right to assume in advance that a candidate of a given religious faith will answer in a given way. Senator Kennedy's answer —already in the record—belies any such simple identification of religious allegiance with any particular point of view on this complicated problem. As will be recalled, the Senator said flatly, "There can be no question of federal funds being used for support of parochial or private schools." For this he was sharply criticized by his own Church's leading journals of opinion; and one journal added that he "will find few Catholics in agreement with his views."

There are other issues; and still others than those now in the minds of Americans may arise before the nomination and election procedures are complete. But whatever the issues, and whoever may be the candidates, we hope that the questions directed to them and the assessment of the answers may be focused in the same spirit in which we have sought to deal with these three more or less presently dormant issues. In short, at the risk of being tiresome about the point, we hope and pray that no man will be discriminated against because of his religion; on the other hand, we hope that the right questions will be asked of *any* candidate whatever his religion—and with no embarrassment because his particular religious faith and its past or present claims may have some relevance to the issues framed by such questions.

CHAPTER EIGHT

Informal Pressures

THE RELATIONSHIP of the Roman Catholic Church to political matters, and her place in American political life, can best be understood in historical perspective. In the closing years of the last century and well into the early part of this one, the Roman Catholic Church was very much the church of the newcomers to our shores. Its part in rural American life was very small, as most of the immigrants tended to settle, at least for one generation, in the larger cities of the eastern seaboard. There were some obvious exceptions to this, of course. In Louisiana, which had been largely settled by Roman Catholic French, the Church had a strong and honored place in the society. This was also true in parts of California, because of its Spanish background, and in the states bordering on old Mexico.

In the East, however, and even more so in the Middle West and the Northwest, Roman Catholics were few and far between, and such as there were tended to stick together. The degree to which this was for ethnic rather than religious reasons is a moot question. In many Eastern communities the Polish, Irish, and Italian congregations seem to have had little to do with one another. The bond between Irishman and Irishman was stronger than the bond between Catholic and Catholic. Nonetheless, to their Protestant neighbors who stood on the outside and attempted to look in, it seemed as though the community of the Roman Catholic Church was a very close one indeed. Until very recently, the majority of Roman Catholic priests were either foreign-born or the children of foreign-born parents and this too added to the strangeness of the Church in the eyes of its Protestant neighbors. In fairness to the Roman Catholic Church, in most places it did well by its foreign-born constituency. Its part in the early days of the labor movement and its real support of its non-English-speaking members stand to its credit in the history of the "melting-pot" experiment.

The "Americanism" Issue

It should be pointed out here that the combination of Roman Catholic and European backgrounds reacted together to make the Church very much feared in some quarters. During the era of unrestricted immigration, the banner of "100% Americanism" attracted many followers. The Know-Nothing Party and the Ku-Klux Klan, in turn, relied upon mistrust of foreigners as much as upon hatred of "Romanism" to rally their supporters. Foreigners were feared because they were Roman Catholics; but Roman Catholics were feared because they were foreigners. It is almost impossible to separate the two elements.

Another factor which began to come to the fore early in the days of the great immigration was the combination of religion and politics in the political machines of the large cities. Many of the bosses and ward politicians were, themselves, Roman Catholics (politics being for them one of the few avenues to success then open). What more natural than that they should turn to their Roman Catholic friends for support in their political activities? The stories of such men as James Michael Curley of Boston remind us that these bosses combined a real benevolence for their charges with a strong sense of practical politics. The result of the almost patriarchal care which they took of the people in their wards was, of course, a strong loyalty to the political causes which these men supported. Since, for the most part, these men were Democrats, there was for many years a correlation in the minds of non-Catholics—and in reality—between the Democratic party and the Roman Catholic Church. The phrase, "Rum, Romanism and Rebellion" had enough truth in its second clause that it could be accepted. The immigrants did tend to vote alike—and usually to vote Democratic. It would be hard to say whether they did this because they were Roman Catholics or whether they did it because the Democratic Party organization was the one which paid attention to them as first-generation Americans.

Whatever the reason, it is undoubtedly true that for several decades it was possible, at least in a limited sense and in some places, to identify the "Catholic vote." The places where this was possible were mostly the big cities. The reasons for it were many—and not simply the religious factor. But the fact remained that a certain number of Irish in Boston or Italians in New York City could be counted upon to vote a certain way and their ward bosses could be depended upon to deliver their vote.

A "Catholic Vote" Today?

As one looks at the political scene today, however, he begins to suspect that the "Catholic vote" is becoming less of a reality. There is, for instance, what might be referred to as a "Catholic vote" in the mill districts of Connecticut. It may well be that these people can be counted upon to vote certain ways in relation to certain questions and, for that matter, can be depended upon to support certain candidates. Recent political history, even in Connecticut, however, suggests that this kind of vote can no longer be counted upon as before. When we turn from the urban society of the East and come West, we find that, for instance, in California there are more Roman Catholic farmers in proportion to the farm population than anywhere else in the United States; yet, Californians in several elections consistently crossed party lines to elect Republican Earl Warren, and the farm vote was strongly in his favor. For that matter, the State of California has only recently elected its first Roman Catholic Governor. Interestingly enough, Governor Brown's weakest support was, by and large, in the farm precincts. The point of this is that Roman Catholic farmers are more apt to vote like farmers than they are to vote like the mill hands of Connecticut who happen also to be Roman Catholics. As the individual members of the Roman Catholic Church become more and more a part of American life, it seems likely that this will become more and more the case. A Roman Catholic farmer in California has far more in common with a Protestant farmer in Iowa than he has with a New England factory worker, despite the fact that the two happen to profess the same faith. It is very likely that, speaking quite objectively, the concept of the "Catholic vote" is becoming less and less valid.

We have already cited (in Chapter One) Professor O'Neill's study of the voting records of Roman Catholic Congressmen in the Eightieth Congress. While, to our knowledge, no such study has been made of United States voters in general, it seems likely that such a study would probably reveal no clear "Catholic position." Dr. Kenneth Wilson

Underwood's *Protestant and Catholic: Religious and Social Inter-action in an Industrial Community*, published in 1957, is unique in its field as perhaps the only serious study of the influence of the Roman Catholic Church on an industrial community. In a chapter entitled "Morality of Politics," Dr. Underwood points out that, despite the preponderance of Roman Catholics in the community which he studied (Holyoke, Massachusetts), a great many factors other than religious played a part in the vote. "The French Catholic candidate for State Senate carries Ward Two not so much because he is French or a Catholic but because he is a Democrat, because he stands for certain social beliefs strongly held in Ward Two, and because he is known in the area and is able to conduct a forceful campaign,"[1] Dr. Underwood concluded.

Even if it is still true in some limited sense to speak of a "Catholic vote," it would be a somewhat less than valuable concept unless one were able to identify the issues which would probably bring this vote into play. It should be quite obvious to any observer that Roman Catholics do not vote as a unit on all political issues, if, indeed, they vote that way on any of them. If it were true, for instance, that all Roman Catholics would vote Democratic, regardless of the issues involved, it is highly doubtful that the Republican party could ever elect a President. Certainly Nelson Rockefeller would not be Governor of New York, a state in which the balance of power could fairly easily be controlled by the Roman Catholics if they did vote as a single group. On the basis of recent elections, it would seem to be far more accurate to speak, for instance, of the "Southern vote" or the "Northern liberal vote" than of the "Catholic vote." It appears, in short, that the Roman Catholic Church has been a strong part of the American scene long enough to be more and more developing various social philosophies within its own framework. The political views of a Dorothy Day or an Ammon Hennacy of the *Catholic Worker* movement are so far from those of a Joseph McCarthy that a lumping of the two together under the phrase the "Catholic vote" is patently ridiculous.

But What of a Presidential Election?

Now it has been seriously questioned, and with good reason, it would appear, whether the "Catholic vote" would unite behind a Roman Catholic for the Presidency. *Newsweek* magazine (December 21, 1959) used its "Listening Post" to ask the question, "How do American Catholics, in general, feel about the prospect of a Roman Catholic candidate for President?" The answers which the column turned up included the following: "He would like to see a Catholic run and win, mainly to wipe out the shibboleth that no Catholic can be elected President of the United States; he would not cast his own vote for that Catholic unless he was convinced that he was the candidate best qualified for the job." *Newsweek* also pointed out that the percentage of Roman Catholic politicians who hoped that a Catholic would not be nominated was higher than the percentage of Roman Catholic voters who hoped the same thing. The article quoted, for instance, former Democratic National Chairman Frank E. McKinney as saying, "It would be a handicap to the entire state ticket in Indiana to have the national ticket headed by a Catholic." Fr. Charles Rice, Pastor of the Immaculate Conception Church of Washington, Pennsylvania, was quoted as saying, "The Catholic people got badly burned in 1928, and I can't see any advantage in stirring up the bitterness again. Personally, I wish that Kennedy wouldn't run."

The point of these quotations seems to be that even in the situation where a "Catholic vote" would seem to be most predictable, namely, a Roman Catholic's running for President, the odds are that no such group voting would materialize. Presumably, staunch Republican Roman Catholics would continue to vote for the Republican candidate, regardless of his church affiliation. Loyal Democratic Roman Catholics, on the other hand, would vote as Democrats rather than as Roman Catholics and, finally, even some of the Roman Catholics—especially among "independents"—could be counted upon to vote against the Roman Catholic candidate for various reasons of their own. One trend of thought, for instance, which *Newsweek* reported was that which said, "If a Roman Catholic candidate is elected, his Roman Catholicism will be blamed for every mistake of his administration." Some Catholics might vote against a Roman Catholic President because they felt this danger to be a real one.

Politicians and the "Catholic Vote"

Yet, on the other hand, the practical politician seems to make almost a fetish of wooing this perhaps nonexistent "Catholic vote." Whether or not it is a reality, it is very greatly respected by men of a practical political turn. President Eisenhower's reaction to the question of foreign aid toward population control discussed in Chapter Six is a good case in point.

Though there are two positive ethical views on the matter of birth control, both of which had been fully spelled out in the preceding days, the President chose to base his position on only one of them, that of the Church representing a minority of our citizens on this question, and remained silent on the other one. Since this "majority" view is held by the Presbyterians, at least we cannot here fault the President for seeking to promote the views of his own Church!

Just a week later, when the President left for his good-will tour of Europe and the Middle East, one of his most important points of call was at the Vatican, for an audience with the Pope. While the President's trip was being planned, some churchmen urged that while in Europe he call upon the Patriarch of Constantinople, head of the Eastern Orthodox Church, most of whose 130 million members live behind the Iron Curtain, around its edge, and in the troubled Middle East. Though the President was to be right in Istanbul his office replied that his schedule would not permit such an interview. Either of the possible calls was pregnant with diplomatic advantages; but apart from the relative diplomatic value, there was doubtless another factor: in this country there are more Roman Catholic voters than Eastern Orthodox voters.

The Roman Catholic Church has good public relations, it may be said to its credit. When one considers that, despite its tremendous membership, it includes less than a third of our citizens, the magnitude of this public-relations program becomes apparent. If a movie or television script calls for someone to seek help in prayer, it is almost invariably to a Roman Catholic church that he goes. If a ministerial part is needed, it is usually a Roman Catholic priest who fills the bill. In fairness to the people who make movies, it is easy to see why this is so. The pictorial values of the externals of the Roman Catholic Church are far superior to those of most of the Protestant denominations. A clerical collar immediately defines the role; a discreet tie doesn't. As for laymen, how does one show a Protestant in prayer? Does he go to his knees in his bedroom, does he read his Bible, does he sit in meditation, or what? But it is easy for the director who wishes to show a Roman Catholic in prayer. He goes to an altar rail and lights a candle. Video is better. The people who make our movies and write our television scripts have simply chosen the easier path. By the same token, the personalities of various Roman Catholic priests have lent themselves to the dramatic medium. Fr. Duffy and his "Fighting 69th"; Fr. Flanagan and his "Boys' Town"; the fictional Fr. O'Malley, played so magnificently by Bing Crosby in Leo Mc-Carey's "Going My Way." Pictures like these have done much to bring about an acceptance of the Roman Catholic Church, and this is all to the good. They have also, however, done some little to magnify the relative importance of the Roman Church in the American scene, in the minds of the unchurched, and even of many Protestants.

Roman Catholic Influence

Since most politicians are not notoriously indifferent to pressures, it is no wonder that they fear and respect the political influence of the Roman Church. The very fact that they do so makes that influence real, even if it remains unwieldy and undirected. Politicians live by votes. They seek them where they are to be found, and they are convinced—correctly or not—that they are to be found "grouped" in the Roman Catholic Church. In view of this, one is tempted to examine the evidences of Roman Catholic influence on public officials.

We have already alluded to Dr. Underwood's definitive study. This work, based upon research in a town referred to as "Paper City" but actually Holyoke, Massachusetts, goes into the question of Roman Catholic influence upon civic life at great length. The first incident cited in the book is what the author refers to as "the Sanger incident."[2] This took place in 1940, when the pastor of Grace Congregational Church agreed to allow Margaret Sanger to use the church buildings for a meeting of the Mothers Health Council at which Mrs. Sanger intended to speak upon the subject of birth control. Here are some of the pressures which were used to prevent her appearance: A prominent banker, who was a member of the Congregational Church was approached, first by a Roman Catholic layman, and later by the Rector of one of the Roman Catholic churches in town. While no actual threat of an economic boycott was apparently used, such a possibility was hinted at by the laymen. The businessman involved in the incident did not accuse the Roman Catholic priest of making any such threat. He did speak to friends, however, of ways in which the Roman Catholic priest could affect his business to its detriment.

At a meeting of the Standing Committee of Grace Church called by the businessman in question, it was decided to rescind the permission granted to the Mothers Health Council to use the church. The meeting was finally held in the meeting rooms of the Textile Workers Union.

The aftermath of this incident brought a number of reactions. At least one member of the Standing Committee resigned because he did not like the idea that "whatever I do or say must be pleasing to the Catholic Bishop of this Diocese." The local *Transcript* carried an editorial attempting to soothe wounded feelings. The editorial said, "Here in Holyoke no one anywhere wants any division among our churches. We have through the years established a high degree of unity among our churches on all civic community problems. We want to hold onto it, to develop it further." The most interesting point of view in the entire matter was that presented by the Roman Catholic priest involved, as reported by Dr. Underwood. He says, "The pastor in his defense of Divine Law feels justified in using economic boycott and says matter-of-factly that he and Monsignor McGuire did use it in the Sanger controversy. He considers a Christian a poor one 'who holds economic or political interest before the maintenance of religious laws' and he asks 'Do Protestants have no religious laws they value so highly they will sacrifice economic or political rights to defend them?' "[3]

This issue, of course, did not directly involve pressures upon city officials. But Dr. Underwood records an incident which did:

> The mayor had co-operated closely with the Catholic church in its gambling program particularly since 1945 when a referendum in the state eliminated beano or bingo from the legal forms of fund-raising activity specifically permitted when the proceeds were for educational, charitable, fraternal and religious purposes. The mayor states that he gave assurances to both the Immaculate Conception and Holy Rosary pastors that the state laws against beano, bingo, and lotteries for raising funds for religious authorities would not be enforced by the local police. The mayor made available rooms in the city hall for the Immaculate Conception church to conduct its beano games, when the attendance overflowed the storeroom rented on the main street by the church for the games. The mayor said of his decision to offer the facilities of the city hall to the Catholic church:
>
> > The priest of Immaculate Conception—an exquisitely beautiful church by the way—is a dear, hard-working fellow. He came to me

one day and said, "Joe we have a debt of $450,000 on our church, and our people are poor. They can't even now meet the interest on it. We have to get funds by a beano program." He wanted to know if it was all right to run a game. Well, I knew there was a State law on the books against it, but "who", I said "is going to enforce it? I'll help you all I can with police and fire department aid." So he said that he could rent a storeroom on High Street. They soon had so many playing we had to open up rooms in the city hall to accommodate them. The first summer, the church cleared $11,000."[4]

The Mayor involved in the above incident, interestingly enough, was himself a Protestant, Dr. Underwood says, as he continues to discuss a controversy which this use of gambling as a fund-raising measure brought on. He continued:

"The only arrest made by the police for gambling violation during the controversy was of a Protestant woman in a local Smith College alumnae association who was selling lottery tickets for the association. (The prize was a trip to Bermuda.) She was fined $25. (Her young daughter at the same time was helping several Catholic girls sell lottery tickets on a doll raffle at Holy Cross parish.)"[5]

Space prevents our citing further examples from his work; but for anyone seriously interested in studying the effects of Roman Catholic influences upon a community in which members of the Roman Catholic faith are in the majority, no book could be more illuminating than Dr. Underwood's treatise.

Naturally, none of us would question the right of Roman Catholics or anyone else legitimately to attempt to seek the help of other citizens or civic officialdom in bringing about those results which they feel to be good. Most of us, however, would seriously question the use of economic sanctions—particularly of the illegal "secondary boycott" type—to do this, and it is the apparent willingness to use such methods which has brought much criticism upon Roman Catholics at the community level.

On the other hand, as one approaches higher levels of government, one seems to find these incidents of direct influence becoming fewer and farther between. Roman Catholic governors, as a group, have often seemed inclined to "lean over backwards" to avoid any charge of favoritism to their Church. While there are undoubtedly incidents in which the Church's pressure has been felt, they are perhaps not nearly so many as some Protestants would imagine.

"Unconscious" Influence

Having said this, however, we should like to point out that one of the most dangerous types of political influence is that wielded by the man who does not recognize that he is wielding it. In many communities one wealthy man holds a great deal of power without bothering to exercise it at all. The community is keenly aware of his presence and of his feelings toward certain subjects. The argument "Mr. So-and-So will be against it" is often sufficient to scotch worthy projects before they get off the ground and without Mr. So-and-So's ever being consulted. Certainly then he can't be blamed for the result. By analogy it is in this sense that the influence of the Roman Catholic Church upon American politicians is not only most effective but most likely to be felt. Yet, this fact is not unique as to the Roman Catholic Church: other religious and non-religious groups in our pluralistic society can have this effect also. Nor would such pressure have an influence on only a Roman Catholic in the White House—or assuming such, would his own church be the only source of consciously or unconsciously felt pressures.

To return to the example of the birth-control incident and President Eisenhower; it is extremely unlikely that any Roman Catholic had put any direct pressure upon Mr. Eisenhower at all. However, knowing what the Roman Catholic position was and being anxious to avoid what he thought was the "group mind" of that religious community, he took a stronger stand in favor of the Roman Catholic position than was either politically necessary or desirable in the national interest in a matter of grave international import. This type of thing is illustrative of what is often a Roman Catholic influence in American politics—without direct pressure.

American Mixed Marriages in Spain

Lest we leave the impression that we feel that all Roman Catholic influence upon high-level government is by indirection only, one example of direct attempt to influence which affected the civil rights of Americans should be cited here. Several years ago, it leaked out that American military authorities had established a policy requiring that an American Roman Catholic and an American non-Roman Catholic, who desired to get married while serving their country in the building and maintenance of our air bases in Spain, must follow the Spanish civil and canon law, the latter requiring as a condition for the dispensation for such marriage that the couple promise that their children would be raised Roman Catholic. It should be noted that this law applied to the case of two American citizens—not merely to an American citizen who wished to marry a citizen of Spain (as to which everyone would agree that Spanish law would have to apply). In this country, of course, the canon law would require the same thing —but any American couple would be free to decide whether they would be married under that law or choose to be married by a clergyman of the non-Roman Catholic party's faith. In short, American personnel temporarily based in Spain were to be deprived of a freedom which was theirs by right as Americans—with permanent effects upon their return to this country.

According to the Roman Catholic chaplain (Colonel Stadka) assigned to negotiate the agreement, the draft had been "initialed" by Cardinal Spellman, of the New York Archdiocese (and Military Vicar for his church). But no word of it had been even breathed to anyone representing the other churches. Interestingly enough, in a telecast the Spanish Ambassador admitted to the wife of one of the present authors that his government had no interest in such a restriction so long as no Spanish citizen was involved. Hence, it was obviously the interest of the Roman Catholic Church—and the Roman Catholic Church in America, at that—that was being favored. Churchmen who attempted to scotch this policy found it difficult enough to do so, although at last they were successful. It might have been much more difficult if we had had at that time a Roman Catholic President who accepted the traditional view of his Church that "error has no rights" or really believed the official position of his Church that such a marriage, if conducted by a Protestant military chaplain, even at the request of both parties, would be "mere fornication."

And so we see there are two problems of influence involved. There is the "unconscious" influence wielded by the Roman Catholic Church through the medium of politicians who consciously seek the Roman Catholic vote. There are also repeated instances of direct influence of the type that we have just cited.

The Inter-Faith Role of the President

There is one further factor which would have considerable bearing upon the ability of a Roman Catholic to serve as President of the

United States. It is perhaps not so important as the others, and yet it could impose a serious limitation upon his abilities to perform at least some of the symbolic duties of his office. Would a Roman Catholic President be limited in the inter-faith nature of his "ministry" to the American people?

One of the authors knows something of this type of role from his experience as Chaplain at Columbia University, in the days of Dr. Eisenhower's presidency. Though a priest of the Episcopal Church, happily in good standing, yet as a University official he was not there *as* an Episcopalian; indeed, the ministry to Episcopal students as such was the responsibility of another priest, who had as his "opposite numbers" clergy of Jewish, Roman Catholic, Presbyterian, Eastern Orthodox and Lutheran persuasions. Time after time he was called upon to participate in inter-faith functions and at the services and meetings of different religious groups, though at no time was he expected to be disloyal to the vows he took at his ordination to the Catholic priesthood by the Episcopal Church. But the reason that this was possible is that his own Church does not regard itself as the only "true Church" and does not regard worship with others—or theological discussion with them—as compromise.

Everyone is aware of the large number of religious and quasi-religious functions in which the President must take part. Seldom a Sunday goes by that the President is not photographed greeting some congregation or other, or at least being greeted by a parson at the door. A Protestant President has often been seen in Jewish and Roman Catholic services and gatherings, taking part as an honored guest and participant. This is as it should be, for the President represents all of the American people and of necessity most of the American people will be of faiths other than his own. While he is not expected to compromise his own faith by preferring one of these others as his own personal religion, or even as regarding all traditions as equally true, he is traditionally expected to take part in a great many affairs which are arranged and sponsored by religious faiths other than his own on an inter-faith basis.

Last winter, while on his "good-will tour" of Middle Eastern and European nations, President Eisenhower desired to take part in a church service in Rome. Special arrangements were made, and he was greeted by the American community at the Protestant Episcopal

Church in that city. In the same week he and his family readily con-
formed to the ceremonial customs surrounding his official audience
with the Pope. His own membership in the Presbyterian Church did
not prevent his taking part in the functioning of other Christian communions. While many people have suggested (and perhaps wisely)
that too many of these things are expected of the President, the fact
remains that they *are* expected and have formed a part of the public
life of the President over the years.

The Roman Catholic Position on Inter-Faith Participation

But *time* for such things would not be the only problem for a
Roman Catholic President. There would also be the position of his
own Church on such matters. It is widely known, although perhaps
not universally, that Roman Catholics are forbidden by the law of
their Church, not only to attend the services of other faiths but are
even forbidden to take part in public (and, for that matter, private)
prayer with individuals of other religious traditions. This is grounded,
of course, in the Roman Catholic position discussed in Chapter Three:
No other "Church" is a Church; "error" has no right to exist. Most
of us have seen this work out in the lives of our Roman Catholic
friends who have been unable without special permission, not always
granted, to take a part in, or even attend, the weddings of close friends
—and even, in some cases, of their own children. While individual
confessors tend to be fairly liberal on this point in the case of weddings
and funerals, particularly of relatives and close friends, the fact remains
that the Church's rule is adamant. Even when special permission is
granted and a Roman Catholic is allowed to attend, he is never granted
permission actually to join in the service, even by so much as repeating
the Lord's Prayer. One does not pray with heretics—and everyone
outside the Roman Catholic Church is a heretic or an infidel.

Some may think that the Roman Catholic Church would make a
blanket dispensation in the case of one of its members who happened
to be President of the United States. This is possible. But let's see the
difficulty from their point of view. How could they continue to "hold
the line" with the average layman in Brooklyn when the most conspicuous Roman Catholic layman in the nation is pictured in the
newspapers at the service marking the long-awaited completion of the
National Cathedral (Episcopal), at the tercentenary of a colonial
synagogue, greeting the World Council of Churches at its next meet-

ing within the United States, or gracing an inter-faith celebration at the anniversary of some historic American shrine of liberty? Obviously such participation would prove a grave embarrassment to the Roman Catholic Church.

A sense of expediency might tempt the appropriate bishop to grant the dispensation; but the same sense of expediency—being sensitive to the possible disillusionment of millions of less conspicuous Roman Catholics—would argue for a denial of the dispensation, or, perhaps more informally, for pressure on the President to find "a way out." The capacity of the Church to do just this is well illustrated by a striking incident reported in Dr. Daniel A. Poling's recent book, *Mine Eyes Have Seen*. It is extremely significant here since, coincidentally, it concerns John Kennedy, one of the prominently mentioned Roman Catholic candidates for Presidential nomination. Mr. Kennedy, in his public statements, has indicated that he feels that there would be no conflict between his Roman Catholic allegiance on the one hand and the demands of the Presidency on the other. However, Dr. Poling's story of the events surrounding the dedication of the Chapel of the Four Chaplains at Temple University suggests that this may not be the case.

Dr. Poling's son, the Rev. Clark Poling, was one of the courageous "four chaplains" who died in the sinking of the troop transport, *Dorchester*. For those who do not remember the moving event, the four chaplains gave away their own life preservers to other members of the crew and went down with the ship with their arms linked and joined together in prayer. The four chaplains included two Protestants, a Rabbi, and a Roman Catholic priest.

According to Dr. Poling, the program for a banquet marking the successful completion of fund raising for the chapel included three speakers, persons of each of the faiths represented by the chaplains. Senator Herbert H. Lehman spoke as the special representative of President Truman and as a member of the Jewish faith. The Hon. Charles P. Taft, then Mayor of Cincinnati and President of the Federal Council of Churches of Christ in the U.S.A., was the Protestant speaker. The third key speaker was to have been John Kennedy, then Congressman from Massachusetts. He, according to Dr. Poling, had graciously accepted the invitation to take part in the program.

Two days before the banquet, Dr. Poling reports:

Mr. Kennedy telephoned me from Washington and said that he would have to cancel his appearance. His Eminence, Cardinal Dougherty of Philadelphia, had requested him not to speak at the banquet and not to appear. The Congressman's distress was obvious as he relayed this information. All but overwhelmed with my disappointment, I reminded Mr. Kennedy that the banquet was a civic occasion, that all faiths were participating and that we were meeting, not in a Protestant Church, but on neutral ground in a hotel. The Congressman replied that he understood all of this and that he had done everything that he could to change the Cardinal's position. His speech was prepared, he said, and he would gladly forward it to me but, as a loyal son of the Church, he had no alternative but not to come. Unquestionably, Mr. Kennedy was grieved as he reported Cardinal Dougherty's decision to me, and unquestionably, also, he was profoundly embarrassed.[6]

Dr. Poling also points out that Cardinal Dougherty not only forbade Mr. Kennedy to attend the service but himself withheld any endorsement of the inter-faith memorial. Finally, he recounts, the Cardinal forbade the then Deputy Chief of Chaplains of the Army, Brigadier General James O'Niell, to take part in the service of dedication, presumably. All of these refusals were, apparently, on the grounds that it was against the canon law of the Church for Roman Catholics to take part in public prayer with their Protestant and Jewish brethren.

Alternative conclusions may be drawn from the events just recounted. It may be that Senator Kennedy believes that the discipline which was laid upon him, as a somewhat junior Congressman, would no longer apply when he was President of the United States. This is an unlikely interpretation, with no support in Roman Catholic doctrine or canon law. It may be that on the other hand, the discipline would still apply, and that Mr. Kennedy (as President) would choose to ignore it. One cannot really think so in respect to the author of *Profiles in Courage*.

Dr. Poling concludes:

Today, though I respectfully read what Senator Kennedy has to say, one thing in his record is unmistakably clear. The Church did claim and exercise authority over him while he was in high public office. I believe that there have been priests, and now are priests of the Roman Catholic Church, who would not have exercised the

Church's authority in this manner, but the fact remains that the authority itself is implicit in the Church, and that at least once John Kennedy of Massachusetts submitted, apparently against his own inclinations and better judgment, to its dictates.[7]

Dr. Poling's account appeared in the press on December 5. On December 7, Senator Kennedy declined to comment on the news stories. But, on December 8, his office issued this terse statement: "Senator Kennedy's office states that the story is inaccurate." Five weeks later (January 15) the Senator made a fuller statement in which he admitted that Dr. Poling's facts "were accurate," but insisted that "the conclusion he drew was inaccurate."

"A few days before the event," Senator Kennedy said, "I learned, as Dr. Poling described it in his book, that I was to be 'the spokesman for the Catholic faith.' [The exact quotation from the book: "a spokesman for his Roman Catholic faith."] . . . I further learned that the memorial was to be located in the sanctuary of a church of a different faith. This is against the precepts of the Catholic Church . . . I felt I had no credentials to attend in the capacity in which I had been asked . . . I informed the Rev. Dr. Poling of my difficulty and told him I would have been delighted to have taken part in any joint memorial to which I was invited as a public officer."

Per contra, Dr. Poling has pointed out that on the program for the dinner Mr. Kennedy was billed only as Congressman from Massachusetts; that the basis on which Mr. Kennedy now says he would have attended was not at the time communicated to him; that the Chapel was not to be a part of the sanctuary of another church, but was to be—and is—in the basement, with its own outside entrance, of a building on the Temple University campus, the main floor of which is used for University convocations, and, on Sundays, for Baptist services.

But all these nice distinctions simply underline the degree to which the style of a Roman Catholic President might well be cramped. It is a telling fact that Charles P. Taft, an Episcopalian, was not inhibited from participation by Cardinal Dougherty's opposite number, Bishop Taitt, nor was Senator Lehman blocked by the Rabbis of Philadelphia. Nor was either concerned as to the need for "credentials" to participate as distinguished citizens in a program arranged according to the quite usual American pattern including Protestant, Roman Catholic and Jewish figures. Since Dr. Poling is not only a distinguished minister but, as editor of the *Christian Herald* for many years, an experienced journalist, one would be especially interested as to what the inaccuracies in the account are. However, the story had a happy ending: for the actual dedication a perhaps equally distinguished Roman Catholic layman, the late General William Francis "Wild Bill" Donovan, who was vice-president of the committee to raise the funds to build the chapel, drove from New York to Philadelphia and appeared on the program with President Truman, who delivered the address of dedication.

In any case, the general position of the Roman Catholic Church on any such matter is clear and can be easily ascertained by anyone. A Roman Catholic President would time and time again be confronted in such situations with a choice between the proper fulfillment of his high office and the confining restrictions imposed by his Church.

The various types of informal pressures and factors illustrated in this chapter should not, of course, for any voter, be the sole factor in determining his choice among candidates for the presidency. But they have their place in the picture.

CHAPTER NINE

A Roman Catholic in The White House?

BECAUSE OF THE NATURE of the issue itself, there will be many who will dissent from one or another of the points made in this book. This is as it should be. But we devoutly hope that no reader will say to his friends that because of this book, he will not vote for a Roman Catholic for President. The most that he can honestly say, if he has read the book carefully, is that he has weighed into his total decision (along with important national and international issues which we have not in the least discussed in this book) the views of Presidential candidates on Church and State issues and that he is prepared to vote for or against a particular American citizen for the Presidency. Our greatest hope is that the reader will have been impressed, in relation to his responsible exercise of the ballot, with the following points:

1. No voter should vote against any candidate simply on the ground of his religion. This is bigotry.

2. So to vote would be to impose a "religious test" contrary to the spirit of the Constitutional prohibition.

3. But a man's religio-ethical outlook does—and should—have a bearing on his decision-making, and a holder of public office is no exception to this. Therefore his likely decisions—or announced policies—on particular questions which are affected by religious orientation, are worthy and suitable subjects for consideration by the electorate.

4. One of the most basic things about the American tradition, which operates in a pluralistic culture, is the relationship of Church and State. Most American citizens—including most Roman Catholics,

we are sure—prefer an equal and free opportunity for all faiths, not only for private worship but for public worship, evangelism, and propagation. As to Protestants, Jews, or secularists who may be candidates, no one thinks of asking about this whole question—this tradition is so well established among them. The matter becomes evident and complicated only in the case of a Roman Catholic candidate.

5. There are two well-supported views within the Roman Catholic Church on this general question, and the question is not an abstract one. Those holding the "official view" maintain that "error has no rights" and that the government when it is feasible should protect the Roman Catholic Church by not allowing to non-Roman Catholics the right to propagandize their views. They would feel that ultimately the public schools should be vehicles of Roman Catholic teaching. Further, they are convinced that the Church—as soon as may be—should receive the official protection and support of public legislation and all the trappings of official status.

6. On the other hand, there is a strong tradition, which we hold the average American Roman Catholic follows consciously or unconsciously, to the contrary. He is perfectly happy to see their Church operate in the "competitive market." They may take a theologically dim view of the rest of us but genially they wish us to have the same "breaks" as they have. Those of them who may know of the Vatican strictures to the contrary, regard them as "dated."

7. All of us have friends of the latter type. Whatever may be the internal inconsistencies of their position, we couldn't care less; that's their problem. But when it comes to the crucial question of the highest office in the nation, some of us can be reasonably concerned as to whether it is really possible for a Roman Catholic—when all the chips are down—to hold such genial views.

8. In this connection there are several collateral considerations. First, these same friends are not as disturbed as we are about the application (there you really see it in action) of the "official view" in countries in which their Church has pre-eminence, and some of them will even say, "What business have these Bible-thumping fellows down there in Colombia, anyway? The people are content with their religion." Second, members of this "liberal" group who are articulate in their position do not seem to plead for "the American way" as finally right but simply as a permissible position within Roman Catholic thought. The serious fact is that those taking the genial position

(which we know they mean most sincerely) are running right up against official declarations of Popes, modern as well as medieval, and, as Roman Catholics they are committed to the doctrine of the infallibility of the Pope and of the necessity of external conformity and "internal assent" even to "noninfallible" declarations. It is not impossible that a Roman Catholic layman in so important a post as the Presidency might be reminded of this basic doctrine of his Church. True, Al Smith, when confronted with the force of certain encyclicals is reported to have said with honest perplexity, "What the hell is an 'enkiklika?'" But it is just possible that had he assumed the office of the Presidency someone might have made it his business to provide the answer to his question.

9. All this is not just an abstract question merely suitable for theological seminars. The fact is that it bears on what are in the life of the country certain basic questions, on which voters may differ in terms of their individual conviction as to the right direction of national policy. Most recently, there has been the foreign aid-birth control issue; but still left as "unfinished business" are the matters of public aid to parochial schools, and diplomatic representation to the Vatican, the degree to which we encourage (through the use of our boundless national resources) foreign governments which practice repressive measures against our fellow Christians, and the role of the United States in the political fortunes of the Vatican vis-à-vis other nations.

10. Then there is the question of assessing to what degree a Roman Catholic President would be subject to various types of informal ecclesiastical pressures, and the degree to which a Roman Catholic President would really be able to enter into the occasions reflecting our pluralistic society—and other questions of a considerable variety, the specific nature of which one could hardly predict at the time one casts one's ballot. On the other hand, as important as all these questions are, there are other very important questions—foreign policy, the approach to the problem of nuclear weapons and their testing, and the corollary questions of general disarmament, the policy of taxation, the approach to labor relations, civil rights, including integration and the proper limits of Congressional investigations. The proportion of the problems we have raised as compared with these other questions will vary in the mind of each voter. But nevertheless the questions we have raised are *real* questions.

In the final analysis a voter faced with the question of casting his vote for a Roman Catholic candidate will have to weigh the degree of his own trust in not only the candidate but in the candidate's Church. He will first, of course, consider the candidate's verbalization as to the part that his religious faith will play in his official decisions. Then he should decide whether or not this position is a tenable one. And more importantly, he will have to decide for himself as to the likelihood of the candidate's real intentions to function in this manner and to be a President of "all the people." Too, he will have to consider the likelihood that his Church will allow him to carry out his own good intentions in this area. We, as outsiders, feel that it would be in the long-term interest of the Roman Catholic Church to allow him so to do within the limits of its doctrinal position; and it may well be that the hierarchy of the Church would appreciate this point.

So in answering the question which supplies the title of this book, we come back to the basic question of trust. This is not the only field in which a candidate's words are not the only criterion. No present Roman Catholic possibility—and we are sure none who will surface in the future—will fail to say, "I'm as good an American as anybody else," etc., etc. The degree to which we can trust such well-meant remarks obviously depends upon the man's record in regard to the issues in this area and on our general trust of him as a person; and, as we have indicated, it depends too on our trust of the Roman Catholic Church itself. And so, in closing, we will answer our initial question as best we can:

A Roman Catholic for President? *It depends.*

The asking of the question is not bigotry. It is the exercise of responsible citizenship.

Notes

[City of publication, publisher, and date of publication are omitted where the book cited appears in the Bibliography.]

CHAPTER ONE—BIGOTRY? A RELIGIOUS TEST?

1. Moore, A *Catholic Runs for President*, p. 176.
2. O'Neill, *Catholicism and American Freedom*, pp. 131ff.
3. *Ibid.*, p. 133ff.

CHAPTER TWO—CHURCH AND STATE

1. *Board of Education v. Barnett*, 319 U.S. 624 (1943), overruling *Minersville School Dist. v. Gobitis*, 310 U.S. 586 (1940).
2. *Atlantic Monthly*, vol. 139, May 1927, p. 728.
3. *America*, vol. 100, March 7, 1959, p. 651.
4. *Life*, Dec. 21, 1959, p. 30.

CHAPTER THREE—THE OFFICIAL VIEW OF THE ROMAN CATHOLIC CHURCH

1. See Blanshard, *Communism, Democracy and Catholic Power*, p. 46.
2. Lamennais, *Affaires de Rome*, p. 418, quoted in Nichols, *Democracy and the Churches*, p. 58.
3. Ryan and Boland, *Catholic Principles of Politics*, p. 317.
4. *Ibid.*, p. 318.
5. *Ibid.*, p. 318–19.
6. *Ibid.*, p. 320
7. *Ibid.*, p. 319.
8. *Ibid.*
9. *The Catholic Register* (Nat'l. ed.), June 19, 1949, quoting Fr. Connell in reply to the position of the Rev. John Courtney Murray discussed in Ch. Four.
10. *The Jurist*, vol. 13, no. 4, Oct. 1953.
11. *Ibid.*

12. Cf. Ottaviani, *Institutiones Iuris Publici Ecclesiastici*, Rome: Typis Polyglottis, 1948.

13. Ottaviani, *Deberes del Estado Catolico con la Religion*, Madrid: n.d., p. 19.

14. *Ibid.*, p. 30.

15. *New York Times*, July 23, 1953.

16. *American Ecclesiastical Review*, Sept. 1950, pp. 173ff.

17. *Ibid.*, Sept. 1950, p. 192.

18. *Ibid.*, May 1954, p. 343.

19. *Civiltà Cattolica*, April 1948.

20. Knox, *The Belief of Catholics*, Garden City: Doubleday, 1958, pp. 187ff.

21. Knox, *The Belief of Catholics*, New York: Sheed and Ward, 1927, p. 143.

22. *L'Osservatore Romano*, Dec. 7–8, 1953; *Civiltà Cattolica*, Dec. 1953, pp. 617ff.

CHAPTER FOUR—AN AMERICAN INTERPRETATION

1. *North American Review*, vol. 189, March 1909, pp. 320ff.

2. *Ibid.*

3. Ireland, John, *The Church and Modern Society*, St. Paul: Pioneer Press, 1905, pp. 117–18.

4. Ireland, John, *op. cit.*, 1:214 quoted in Cross, *The Emergence of Liberal Catholicism in America*, p. 81.

5. *Theological Studies*, June 1951, pp. 164–65, vol. 12.

6. *Ibid.*, p. 162.

7. *Ibid.*, p. 155.

8. *Ibid.*, p. 157 (author's footnote).

9. *Ibid.*, p. 173.

10. *Op. cit.*, 14, June 1953, pp. 179–80.

11. Washington: National Catholic Welfare Conference, 1948.

12. "The Catholic Church in American Democracy," Jan. 26, 1948, N.C.W.C. Office of Information.

13. *Commonweal*, vol. 58, Aug. 7, 1953.

14. *Cross Currents*, vol. 5, Winter, 1951, pp. 6ff.

15. *Ibid.*, vol. 5, Fall, 1951, pp. 1ff.

16. *The New Republic*, June 8, 1959, pp. 10ff.

CHAPTER FIVE—SOME DIFFICULTIES

1. *Theological Studies*, 10, Sept. 1949, p. 430.

2. For the quotations in this section from Fr. Murray, see Ch. Four, n. 5.

3. *America*, Dec. 12, 1959, pp. 353–54.

4. *Life,* Dec. 21, 1959.
5. See Nichols, *Democracy and the Churches,* p. 105.
6. *Catholic Encyclopedia,* vol. XIV, p. 368f.
7. Cited in Fremantle, *The Papal Encyclicals in their Historical Context,* p. 27.
8. *America,* April 30, 1957.

CHAPTER SEVEN—DEAD ISSUES—MORE OR LESS

1. Stock, *United States Ministers to the Papal States,* pp. 2f., quoted in Stokes, *Church and State in the United States,* vol. II, pp. 88–89.
2. *Ibid.,* pp. 258f., quoted in Stokes, *op. cit.,* vol. II, pp. 89f.
3. Cross, *The Emergence of Liberal Catholicism in America,* pp. 179ff.
4. *Washington Post,* March 6, 1939.
5. White House press release, Dec. 23, 1939, p. 1, quoted in Stokes, *op. cit.,* vol. II, p. 98.
6. Cf. *Pierce v. Society of Sisters,* 268 U.S. 510 (1925); *Meyer v. Nebraska,* 262 U.S. 390 (1923).
7. But some doubt would seem to be cast on the constitutionality of the plan by dicta in *Everson v. Board of Education,* 330 U.S. 1 (1947) and by the holding in *McCollum v. Board of Education,* 333 U.S. 203 (1948). But cf. *Zorach v. Clauson,* 343 U.S. 306 (1952), by which time the "tone" of the Court's attitude had somewhat altered.

CHAPTER EIGHT—INFORMAL PRESSURES

1. Underwood, *Protestant and Catholic: Religious and Social Interaction in an Industrial Community,* p. 296.
2. *Ibid.,* pp. 3ff.
3. *Ibid.,* pp. 35–36.
4. *Ibid.,* pp. 325f.
5. *Ibid.,* p. 327.
6. Poling, *Mine Eyes Have Seen,* p. 257. New York: McGraw-Hill, 1959.
7. *Ibid.,* p. 261.

Selected Bibliography

Bates, M. Searle, *Religious Liberty: An Inquiry*. New York: International Missionary Council, 1945.

Bennett, John C., *Christians and The State*. New York: Scribners, 1958.

Blanshard, Paul, *American Freedom and Catholic Power*. Boston: Beacon Press, 1949.

Blanshard, Paul, *Communism, Democracy and Catholic Power*. Boston: Beacon Press, 1951.

Blanshard, Paul, *God and Man in Washington*. Boston: Beacon Press, 1960.

Cross, Robert D., *The Emergence of Liberal Catholicism in America*. Cambridge: Harvard University Press, 1958.

Fremantle, Anne, ed., *The Papal Encyclicals and Their Historical Context*, with an Introduction by Gustave Weigel, S.J. New York: New American Library, 1956.

Hales, E. E. Y., *The Catholic Church in the Modern World, A survey from the French Revolution to the Present*. Garden City: Hanover House, 1957.

Herberg, Will, *Protestant-Catholic-Jew: An Essay in American Religious Sociology*. Garden City: Doubleday, 1954.

Knox, Ronald, *The Belief of Catholics*. Garden City: Doubleday, 1958 (1st ed. New York: Sheed and Ward, 1927).

Moore, Edmund A., *A Catholic Runs for President: the Campaign of 1928*. New York: Ronald Press, 1956.

Nichols, James Hastings, *Democracy and the Churches*. Philadelphia: Westminster Press, 1951.

O'Neill, James M., *Catholicism and American Freedom.* New York: Harpers, 1952.

Pelikan, Jaroslav, *The Riddle of Roman Catholicism.* Nashville: Abingdon, 1959.

Pfeffer, Leo, *Church, State and Freedom.* Boston: Beacon Press, 1953.

Ryan, John A., and Boland, Francis J., *Catholic Principles of Politics; The State and the Church.* New York: Macmillan, 1950.

Scharper, Philip, ed., *American Catholics: A Protestant-Jewish View,* with an afterword by Gustave Weigel, S.J. New York: Sheed and Ward, 1959.

Shuster, George N., *The Catholic Spirit in America.* New York: Dial Press, 1927.

Stokes, Anson Phelps, *Church and State in the United States,* 3 vols. New York: Harpers, 1950.

Underwood, Kenneth Wilson, *Protestant and Catholic: Religious and Social Interaction in an Industrial Community.* Boston: Beacon Press, 1957.

Weigel, S.J., Gustave, *Faith and Understanding in America.* New York: Macmillan, 1959.

Index